Real Love

Real Love

WHAT IT IS, AND
HOW TO FIND IT

Theodore Isaac Rubin, M.D.

CONTINUUM · NEW YORK

1990

The Continuum Publishing Company
370 Lexington Avenue
New York, NY 10017

Printed in the United States of America

Library of Congress Cataloging-in-Publication Data

Rubin, Theodore Isaac
    Real love : what it is, and how to find it / Theodore Isaac
Rubin.
        p.   cm.
    ISBN 0-8264-0453-7
    1. Love.   2. Interpersonal relations.   I. Title.
BF575.L8R83   1990
152.4′1—dc20   89-22109
                                                                    CIP

For our beloved young lovers
Jorin and Eugene Rubin
and
all other loving people whatever their age

Real Love

Generates

Real Love!

When we love
we are in touch with the deepest aspects
of our selves and each other.

In a way this gives us special vision of one another's innermost depths, each other's moods, vulnerable areas, needs, joys, and satisfactions. Even the most subtle qualities and gestures have meaning. We see, know, and feel at the same time; a gesture, the quality of voice, a change in walk, the beginnings of a fleeting smile, pain, joy, and much else that cannot be put into words but which is felt and to which we respond.

In this way love brings us exquisite perception and the opportunity for responses and exchange that, without love, never take place. The development of this special sensitivity increases our ability to communicate, adding to love's language and to love itself.

Love, I believe, is the most human emotion

and that is why there is hope for us all.

Love is the most complex, mysterious, and difficult of the human emotions to understand. Definitions don't help.

But we can talk about love and in this way convey something of what it is and what it does.

Love is the most human emotion because it most tells us what it is to be a person in the deepest part of ourselves. This is the part in which we deal best with ourselves and other people. Relating is the very essence of being human.

Some people believe that hate and aggression most characterize the state of being human. I do not! Anger, short-lived warm anger, is quite human. Hate, the chronic thing and aggression are not inborn, instinctual characteristics. They are aberrations and the result of hurt, sick pride.

Love comes from all that is healthy in us. In healthy conditions, love flows as naturally and spontaneously as breathing does.

In fact, our need to love is as great as our need to breathe and it does for our psyches and inner selves what clean air does for our lungs.

The healing power of love—emotionally, mentally, physically, and in relationships—is enormous. Fortunately, our potential for love is enormous too.

Understanding this emotion, the blocks that stand in its way, its effects, and its many shapes and routes help to activate our potential for love. The better we understand love, the better we understand ourselves, each other, and what it means to be a person. Love increases our desperately needed humility and humanity. Only love stands in the way of deadly aggression born of malignant pride.

Hopefully *Real Love* will help in this endeavor because in the final analysis love saves us, love is our great hope for peace—and ultimately our species will survive because of it.

But real love begins within each of us.

It is a reality we must contemplate, understand, and then express "on the spot where we're standing." This book is an endeavor to share with you some ideas that have come to my attention as I've listened and tried to be of help to others very much like you and me during the past thirty years. I've learned that it is not a cliché to view love—unconditional, inclusive, and with no strings attached—as an antidote to much of our suffering, and as the clearest sign of human health and happiness. But real love has many shadings and many colors. Please consider the pages that follow a kind of photo album of one man's learnings on love gleaned over many years as a psychiatrist and as a human being: verbal snapshots of insights and reflections that are both simple and potentially powerful. The book is arranged so that you may read from the beginning or skip around at leisure and rest on those ideas that seem most relevant or helpful at the time.

Real love begins within each of us. If only a page, only a sentence, of *Real Love* sparks the infinite power of love within you, I will be most grateful.

Love is a natural feeling

and every human being is born with the potential to truly love himself and his neighbor. When this doesn't happen it is because unnatural events, actions, deprivations, and assaults have gotten in the way.

When conditions are at all natural and good, love flourishes.

Love gets a special boost when constructive or loving events take place.

People engaged in good work often come to love each other.

People in the process of helping one another or someone else may have to offer considerable resistance to stop love from happening.

Creative enterprise often brings on feelings of love.

Children in our presence can stimulate dormant love feelings in ourselves. The same is true of baby animals.

The goodness of good wholesome food, good clean air, beautiful paintings, flowers, the sea, mountains, and likewise the moon, stars, sky, and the vastness of the universe can help to put us back in touch with a natural flow of love feelings—*if* we only let it happen.

What about loving God and what about faith?

To me, loving God is loving the universe and everything in it.

Having faith is loving the human condition, each other, and believing in the worth and survival of our species.

Loving God and having faith also mean having the humility to know that there is order and meaning in all things even though this is beyond my comprehension. It also means loving the mystery, the unknown of the universe, and seeing myself and my fellows as only a minute part of it but important because we are part of the mysterious whole.

Meet some of love's children.

productivity	praise	affection	respect
loyalty	compassion	responsibility	health
courage	sensitivity	joy	beauty
altruism	support	aliveness	sex appeal
understanding	sharing	energy	charisma
hope	creativity	interests	involvement
peace	contentment	warmth	comfort
honesty	tolerance	generosity	responsibility
awareness	friendship	protection	freedom
sportsmanship	good manners	graciousness	fairness

and the desire to struggle to understand other people's point of view.

Love's enemies unfortunately abound.

It is very important to be able to recognize and to understand them so that we can combat, dilute, and nullify their effect before they become chronic and obliterate the most valuable asset we have. People seldom have full conscious awareness of these corrosives to love. This makes them even more dangerous. People are usually aware of lack of love and misery but are unaware of the corrosives blocking and destroying their loving ability.

Love's enemies are seldom present individually. They are all cousins and are usually present in combination, feeding and supporting each other in undermining love.

I will list love's most common enemies or corrosives here and then I'll discuss each of them at different points throughout the text.

Love's enemy

\# 1—jealousy

\# 2—envy

\# 3—possessiveness

\# 4—projection (and displacement)

\# 5—recrimination

\# 6—sullen silence and abused reactions

\# 7—suspiciousness and paranoia

\# 8—arbitrary rightness

\# 9—arrogance

\#10—greed and stinginess

\#11—getting even or the need to get even

\#12—manipulation

\#13—hidden agendas

\#14—pride

\#15—duplicity and dishonesty

\#16—competitiveness

#17—secretiveness

#18—rejection, vindictiveness, and vengeance

#19—refusal to listen

#20—narcissism

#21—perfectionism

#22—claims

#23—cynicism, pessimism, bitterness, chronic distrust, and
    hopelessness

#24—gossip and the betrayal of confidences

#25—chronic, inappropriate, and gratuitous criticism

#26—mastery

#27—detachment, inattention, and neglect

#28—self-effacement and the compulsive need to be universally
    loved all the time

#29—hate

#30—lies

#31—I want what I want when I want it.

"If only I had told him."

I have so often heard people say they would give anything to tell a parent, particularly a father, that they love him.

But tragically he is gone and it is too late.

I wonder how many of them would have been able to do it when he was alive if he had said it to them when they were growing up.

In our macho-oriented society

when a father weeps openly in response to being deeply touched in front of his children, he is giving them a gift of love.

Few people

remain unmoved by genuine expressions of love.

People who are not moved have forgotten how to love themselves and others.

Sex

can be loving and most intimate and a repeated statement of commitment, but it can also be cold, prefunctory and mechanical, bitter and hostile, and a way to stay emotionally removed and distant.

Some people have sex in order not to talk and to avoid any kind of exchange of feelings or giving of self. The sexual act here has no relationship to commitment, not even for the time it takes to complete the sex act.

I am convinced that most heart attacks and strokes that occur during sex happen in sexual activity that is essentially bitter and hostile.

I remember interviewing hundreds of prostitutes when I was the psychiatrist at the New York City House of Detention many years ago.

They had no feeling about sexual intercourse. But they had very strong feelings about kissing on the mouth and "real hugging that means something." These were reserved for lovers *only!*

But they said something else too. They said that most of their clients would not come to them at all if their wives were willing to participate as often and in the ways the men desired. I believe this was partially true. I believe that most of the men would not frequent prostitutes if sex with wives and lovers was of the loving intimate kind.

Love's enemy #1: jealousy.

What makes this corrosive particularly deadly and insidious is the extent to which it is misrepresented in our society. This is such a prevalent and bad one that we better take a good look!

This prime enemy to love actually hides under the mantle of being evidence of love, the very substance of which it blocks and destroys.

Make no mistake about it! Jealousy is narcissistic, greedy selfishness in purest form. Jealousy is never proportional or even related to love.

"I loved her so much I was constantly jealous" is a much-heard phrase. It is pure hokum. "I was so sick, infantile, and self-consumed and full of jealousy I couldn't love her, myself, or anyone else" is much more consistent with the truth.

Jealousy is the inappropriate and unwarranted fear that something we own or believe we own and think we need will be taken from us. You can see at once that jealousy is linked to stifling possessiveness. It comes from exaggerated, sick, and usually hidden (from the jealous person) dependency, feelings of inadequacy, and the fear of being unable to stand on one's own two feet. Overprotectiveness in early childhood and the subsequent unconscious continuing fear of parental abandonment displaced to so-called loved ones in adulthood accounts for much chronic jealousy.

Jealousy is the direct result of long-standing or temporary feelings of unlovability or unworthiness. In effect, the jealous person feels "If I don't love me—how can she? If she finds out the truth about how nothing I am, she will abandon me. At best, my hold on her is fraudulent and tenuous and in constant jeopardy. Anyone is worthier than me and if she finds this out or if he just comes along or if she finds out how needy and greedy I am I will lose her and my self-hate will be devastating."

Acute attacks of jealousy often follow any occurrence that knocks down self-esteem. These include business failures, poor exam grades, sexual difficulties, sickness, aging—especially in our society, the arrival of each decade birthday, etc. In chronic jealousy, long-standing feelings of inadequacy going back to childhood are usually easy to recognize.

Reassurance of lovability doesn't help unless the root problems involving insecurity and poor self-esteem are addressed and resolved. Evidence of caring, fidelity, and support change nothing at all. Psychotherapy, especially in chronic cases, may be necessary.

Love simply cannot flourish where jealousy exists. What is sometimes at first seen as flattering soon becomes a monstrous, constricting nightmare leading to accusations and corrosive, vindictive mutual destruction.

*People who love each other respect
their individual preferences and
the need to be alone now and then.*

Chronic togetherness is evidence of morbid dependency rather than love.

But lovers also have the capacity, urge, and satisfaction of doing much together. This includes work, problem solving, and especially play and fun.

Spouses and lovers who exclude their mates from problem areas often rationalize that they are saving them from pain and worry. This is usually an excuse for maintaining distance or sustaining a macho image. Is is really evidence of an inability to share and eventually erodes the ability to have pleasure together, too.

There is no substitute for fun together—shared laughter. This is one of the best vehicles for love. It is both an expression of love as well as an enhancer of love.

In short, shared experiences of all kinds aid the love process. This includes difficulties as well as fun times. But there are times when being alone is appropriate also.

especially by people with long-standing relationships may at times convey messages of love more than words and more than gifts.

This may or may not have an erotic effect.

But, words—saying it in so many words—is a more certain way of conveying feelings.

Actions—doing loving things that indicate great consideration and care—are evidence of love but may not convey the message as well as affectionate words and touching. But actions have more of a staying effect in sustaining the love message.

The combination of all of the above—the actualities of efforts expended for love and the symbols: words, touch, and thoughtful gifts—is most powerful in conveying and sustaining the message.

Despite the songs

that whine on about the frustration, desperation, sadness, and pain of love, I believe love is mostly good feelings, good health, aliveness, joy, and just plain fun.

Being in love with love can be
dangerous on several accounts.

1. It can lead to disasterous commitments and decisions. Wishful thinking does not constitute the real thing! I'm all for giving a relationship a chance, but there is little as dangerous as impulsive decisions and action based on desperate desire.

The preventive here is to get to know each other before commitment takes place. This always requires time for which there is no substitute—however perceptive or intuitive we may be.

2. Being in love with love often leads to fickle desires and behavior adding confusion to confusion.

3. Being in love with love always leads to exorbitant expectations. However much two people are in love:

a. They sometimes have different tastes and desires.

b. Misunderstandings do take place.

c. Outside problems do impinge and create stress.

d. Kids and adults too develop problems—like sickness, school, lack of money, etc.

e. People have their limitations. Mortality remains a fact of life.

f. Every wish and need cannot be fulfilled.

g. Every communication cannot be understood.

In this connection, I want to say that reality is a great friend of love—sustained love. To the extent that we know what it is to be a person, continuing love is favored.

Simple facts are: People are sometimes confused, jealous, envious, stingy, generous, helpful, helpless, courageous, afraid, cowardly, tempted, good, bad, indifferent, involved, healthy, conflicted, sick, prideful, humble, unfortunately hateful, and fortunately loving, too. These and countless other characteristics are common in each and every one of us and the capacity to love makes it all somewhat easier but never perfect.

No one is perfect.

No relationship is perfect. The value of apology cannot be exaggerated.

The ability to admit to being wrong is indication of acceptance of being human. It helps immeasurably to combat deadly and painful pride deadlocks.

To be wrong, to accept it, to be sorry but nonrecriminating for wrongdoing is a relief to all concerned. It paves the way to go on, having learned from mistakes so as to make further transactions better.

Forgive and forget! This is pure gold. However much we love—mistakes, hurts, indiscretions are inevitable. We must forgive ourselves. We must forgive each other. Forgiveness is evidence that apology has value—that it has been accepted and appreciated, so that we can move on constructively.

But forgiveness without forgetting is not forgiveness at all—only an empty gesture. Forgiveness is the real thing only when we struggle and succeed in putting the hurt behind us. This makes us truly free of it so that it does not impede our love—much as a pebble in a shoe hurts the foot with each step taken.

Helping people

to help themselves is love.

Helping them in ways that increase their helplessness is neither love nor help. It is invariably a contribution to one's own self-aggrandizement.

*There are people
who invariably make us feel
a little better each time we talk to them
or are in their presence.*

I believe they have the special gift to make us feel better about ourselves—to make us more self-accepting.

I don't know if they have this effect on everyone.

But I surely know this is a form of love and those of us who benefit from it are receiving love—one of the best kinds.

Love's enemy #2: envy

is self-corrosive and fatal to relationships, especially with people we
envy. Eventually this includes just about everyone. It is an absolute,
thorough killer of love feelings.

Always wanting what other people have or seem to have makes it
impossible to love those people or to receive love from them.

The source of envy is much the same as that of jealousy—coming
from feelings of impoverishment and reactive insatiability. Envy
tends to be chronic. Jealousy can come in short attacks but envy
tends to be a condition that, once it takes hold, remains malig-
nantly entrenched. When jealousy is chronic we nearly always find
envy present, too. Thus the victims of these two malevolent forces
are frightened that something or someone will be taken from them
and will always want what someone else seems to have.

Of course, envious people feel whatever they have is worthless.
They never feel they have enough, are never happy with what they
have, and never believe or feel the love they get is either real or
sufficient.

Humor

is an enormous aid especially when communicating is difficult for whatever reason. It lightens the pressure of frustration.

But compulsive joking is a way of keeping distance by not allowing true feelings to come through. This is destructive to communication and love.

Love

of selves, others, *the one and only,* does not mean liking all aspects or everything that comes up.

But it does mean acceptance of the total person and loyalty—through thick and thin, in youth and advanced age, with assets, limits, and idiosyncrasies.

Of course this kind of self-acceptance and acceptance of each other is much easier if there is little or no idealization and inhuman or superhuman expectations in the first place.

Trying to teach without love

is usually extremely frustrating, fatiguing, and more often than not unsuccessful.

Effective teaching invariably takes place with love and produces still more love.

1. Love of teaching.
2. Love of learning. Teachers—real teachers—always learn from their students.
3. Love of the subject.
4. Love of the student.
5. Love of the teacher.
6. Love of healthy change and growth.
7. Love of creative seeds germinating and coming to fruition.
8. Love of people.
9. Love of uniqueness or individuality.
10. Love of humor.
11. Love of patience and the effective use of talent, time, energy, and perseverance.

Since ordinary communication is also a form of teaching—in which we explain and exchange points of view—we can readily see the importance of love in this connection.

Sexual selfishness

as with all selfishness is a problem in love/sex relationships that must be worked out to prevent destructive unhappiness.

The particular difficulty here is that many parties simply do not know that they are selfish in this area. They must be told! Keeping peace at any price is a disaster! Not wanting to hurt pride is a disaster.

In fact, feelings are being hurt—the feelings of the person being deprived. Also, the love relationship is being hurt because selfishness prevents the development of full amplitude of shared sex, shared feelings, and shared experiences in all areas of life. It also contributes to chronic dissatisfaction, frustration, anger, and subtle passive/aggressive sabotage of the relationship. Of course all of these repercussions cripple the possibility of full satisfaction by all concerned.

Of course how the telling takes place in this delicate area is crucial. It must not be done so subtly that the message fails to be conveyed. But gentleness, compassion, and every indication of willingness to cooperate—including seeking professional help if necessary—go a long way here.

Love's enemy #3: possessiveness

invariably leads to distrust, suspiciousness, and to constriction—the antithesis of love. "I love you so much I never want to let you out of my sight" has less to do with love than morbid dependency and exploitation.

Chronic possessiveness denigrates a loved one (adult or child), who becomes a possessed object rather than a respected, dignified, separate, and whole human being.

This enemy of love is always linked to infantile needs and lack of development and just plain growing up. Profound insecurity is present here.

Highly possessive people rationalize this disability with protestations of great love. Their attitudes demean love and sustain selfish, neurotic drives that must be treated through insight and the struggle to live (as an adult) and to let live, otherwise love will wither.

Love between parent and child
is the enzyme that makes
the child grow emotionally.

This may well apply physically as well as emotionally. Pediatri-
cians have recently demonstrated that little boys deprived of mother
love do not generate sufficient growth hormone. They remain
stunted. But they are cured and grow by leaps and bounds when
love is provided through a loving foster mother.

Adults have the same response on an emotional and intellectual
level. Love is the catalyst that makes for the stimulating exchange
that makes growth possible.

Self-love

is the antithesis of self-inflation, self-aggrandizement, self-glorification, and selfishness that is greedy self-concern to the exclusion of others.

In real and healthy self-love we always care about others, too, because this more than anything in life nourishes the self. Exclusion of interest in others results in self-decay.

Self-love means real self-care. This includes health, interest in life, and the development of talents and natural abilities. It also means the avoidance of counterproductive activities (drugs, smoking, disastrous relationships, etc.). But above all, self-love means wherever possible changing dislike to like and hate to love.

The simple fact is that loving things, activities, anything, and especially people feels good and feeling good is good for us. Indeed, it is probably the best overall medicine that exists.

The man told me this about love and himself.

"I don't know how to receive it."
"I don't know how to give it."
"I just don't know how to handle it."
I told him that first he must recognize it. Then he must allow himself to feel it more and more. The rest would follow.

Q. "Why did you marry him?"

A. "He loved me so much I couldn't resist."

Q. "But you are so unhappy. There seems to be nothing you have in common."

A. "It's true and I knew it from the start. But when he said he loved me all other considerations went out the window."

Unfortunately this is a real dialogue and the "he loved me so" motivation for commitment is all too common. It is particularly prevalent among people who feel so unlovable that they are particularly vulnerable and sensitive to any sign of being loved and who overreact to anything that can be interpreted as being loved.

These people (in our society—mostly women) are in love with love. They are very dependent people and desperate to be loved.

They confuse the man's infatuation (often sexual) and their own need to be loved with real love. They see themselves as being of so little importance that how they really feel carries no weight at all in their decisions. Therefore, the fact that they don't love the man doesn't enter into the decision at all since what they feel has no relevance.

So many of these people have little or nothing in common other than powerful, unrequited needs.

Since feelings are not exchanged, the man's crush soon turns to ashes and even the small satisfaction of being told of being loved is denied the woman. In this circumstance the relationship becomes counterproductive and fails.

When lovers become angry

it is important that they tell each other what they are angry about. The sooner the information is exchanged the better. This prevents distortion, exaggeration, confusion, and misunderstanding.

"Fighting"

is constructive when it is about issues and destructive when its goal is to put each other down.

Optimism

aids love's cause immensely. An outlook that invites the possibility of good things happening prevents our love-generating feelings from running down and rusting away.

Of course, pessimism has the opposite destructive effect. It keeps the door so tightly closed that good things aren't recognized and can't get in however loud they knock.

Love is the binding stuff
of brotherhood and sisterhood.

When we empathize, sympathize, care—even as we remain ourselves—in effect we exchange places with the other person. We at
least in part feel what he or she feels—his pain, her joy. In this
regard we exchange aspects of each other and are enriched by the
process.

Morbid dependency is not the same thing at all! This process is
depleting rather than enriching. Instead of free giving of self—there
is dilution of self in the attempt to absorb the other person.

The thing about love is that the exchange results in a change, but
always an enriching, self-fulfilling change.

Love's enemy #4:
projection (and displacement)

is terribly destructive to fruitful communication and invariably leads to rage, accusations, bitterness, and confusion—all of them love cripplers. Even worse, projection can become chronic suspiciousness and paranoia.

Projection is the process of blaming the other person for one's own difficulties. Displacement is the process of shifting blame and anger from one person or event to another. John is enraged with his boss and shifts his anger to his wife. These mechanisms, as many of love's enemies, usually go on unconsciously even though rage and distrust are usually felt consciously.

When two people engage in these processes confusion reigns supreme. Since they both abdicate responsibility they make constructive change very difficult if not impossible.

Lovability.

Over the years, particularly when I wrote regular magazine columns, I was asked and wrote about lovability—really being lovable.

What Are Some of the Major Common Attributes Found in Real Lovability?*

1. An ability to be direct about expressing feelings, desires, goals, dislikes, hurts—no subtle manipulative messages here.
2. Good frustration tolerance and a willingness to struggle to communicate—both in listening and explaining.
3. The willingness to learn and to teach, especially about demonstrations of affection and sexual activity.
4. A tolerance and respect for other people's differences of opinions, values, interests, tastes, and goals.
5. Kindness in any form whatsoever.
6. Love of self as demonstrated by good self-esteem, acceptance and compassion as well as healthy self-care physically, mentally, intellectually, and in the enhancement of one's own attractiveness.
7. Love of people and the human condition as well as nature and the respect for life.
8. Sensitivity and care for other's moods, problems, whims and needs.
9. The ability to receive and to give graciously.
10. The ability to say "I am wrong" and to be able to apologize without hurt feelings or acrimony of any kind.

*Most of us have at least some of them. Some of us have most of them.

11. A capacity for appreciation and gratitude.

12. A capacity for joy in other people's accomplishments and joys.

13. A fair degree of independence.

14. A sense of humor and an ability to have fun, to laugh, and to be openly affectionate.

15. The ability to be sad, to be able to weep as well as to be able to be openly angry and to be openly vulnerable.

16. The ability to show the need and to ask for support and help without hurt-pride reactions.

17. The ability to live in the present.

18. The ability to make bad moods short and to bounce back.

19. The ability to assume responsibility and to make mistakes without generating guilt in self and others.

20. Minimal self-hate and projection and claims.

21. The desire, readiness, and joy in praising others.

22. The ability to emote easily and to be enthusiastic, excited, and responsive.

23. Open looks—the kind that show feelings—the opposite of the poker face.

24. The obvious enjoyment of kindness received and given as well as generosity of spirit and the enjoyment of ordinary goodness and good things like fresh air, food, birds, animals, kids, music, talk, etc.

25. Optimism.

26. The ability to love in any and all manifestations.

27. Humility (never to be confused with humiliation) in which we are in touch with real assets and real limits.

Love dissipates the poison
of malice.

Love is a natural cleanser of the human psyche.

Once love gets rooted it grows, spreads, and destroys jealousy, envy, greed, vindictiveness, and all the other unnatural enemies of the mind and body.

But we must give it a chance to root and flourish by recognizing and standing against those enemies as a starting point. Once love has flourished for a while, it cleanses the psyche and aids in the healing process on all levels.

*Of course people express love
in different ways and that's OK.*

But if love is expressed or demonstrated so subtly that no one picks it up then it surely needs change and amplification.

Put simply—*Turn it up!*

"I love you"

is said every time and in every way that we show that you are not alone.

When we say,"I am with you," or indicate it in any way by our deep attention, presence, support, we are saying, "I love you."

Only love can save us.

Love alone can neutralize psychotic national pride, psychotic greed, crippling aggression, and species annihilation.

Love's enemy #5: recrimination

is demoralizing, stultifying, invites at worst retaliatory recrimination, and at best guilty defensiveness.

Recrimination is always nonproductive! It never aids love!

It makes for bitterness, hurt feelings, helplessness, and is an antilove mechanism par excellence.

To the extent that we can avoid being judgmental we can prevent recrimination because being judgmental is nearly always the preamble to this destructive tearing down.

When something goes awry between people, the adult, constructive, and loving thing to do is to try to analyze with compassion what the situation is all about and to take effective remedial steps.

Judgment and recrimination are the stuff of hate and punishment.

Insight, exploration, and nonjudgmental help are expressions of people who love each other. Forgiving and forgetting are crucial to love.

Still better is the acceptance of foibles and mistakes in the first place so that forgiveness is not even necessary and recrimination is excluded altogether.

When two people marry

and both of them have had parents who loved each other they have an enormous advantage in their future love lives.

But those of us who have not had this great advantage almost always have the capacity to struggle for the samè excellent love lives together.

Love sometimes happens quickly.

Sometimes it happens slowly.

But for me there is no question that love grows with the passage of time—if it is the real thing.

As I've said in other places—shared history (and we create personal history together as time goes on) makes relationships special.

However much we love each other,
the beginnings of living together
can pose problems.

This is not evidence of having made a mistake, serious irreconcilable differences, or lack of love. It only means that a period of adaptation, adjustment, and accommodation is necessary. Patience, compassion, respect for differences are highly valuable commodities here.

The early period of being together must not be viewed as a test of love. If it is any test at all, it is a test of our ability to struggle to live as healthy, relating adults. This always takes time. If we expect instant adjustment, serious disappointment will follow.

This period of initial adjustment (actually our entire lives require constant adjustments and this constitutes growth) applies to the honeymoon and its equivalent. Honeymoons are characterized by anxiety, high expectations, fatigue, valleys following wedding emotional highs, solitude with each other after being with a great many people, and being in strange and unfamiliar places. Sometimes "lovemaking" can be fun despite these conditions. Sometimes it can be difficult and may even not be desired. In any case, these intense romantic periods—initiating being exclusively together—must not be looked upon as either mandatory in themselves (we don't need to go away) or in the responses we are supposed to have.

A honeymoon can be fun if our expectations are minimal, our *shoulds* and *shouldn'ts* are minimal, and we refuse to regard any initial period together as a test of any kind.

Love's enemy #6: sullen silence and abused reactions

go together and destroy communication and undermine love.

The "hurt" partner here feels abused and caters to this feeling—feeding it and prolonging it as much as possible.

In a perverse way, this makes him feel like a superior, misunderstood, virtuous martyr, and this serves as proof (only to him) that he was right after all.

In order to sustain the belief of being unappreciated and abused and to hurt the supposed grievance producer, he will sulk in silence.

This both prevents any remedy to take place and frustrates the partner who usually has no idea what indiscretion, if any, has been committed.

The *sulker* hopes in this way to engender sufficient guilt so as to have his way in future dealings. The ultimate effect is to produce frustration and rage, ultimately destroying communication vital to love.

"Live and let live."

What does this mean?

It certainly should not be construed as an argument for uncaring detachment!

The way I see it, to people who love, this means respect for each other's individuality and differences.

There is no attempt to inundate, prosyletize, or to pressure, even though there may be a lively exchange of ideas. Differences in tastes, appetites, and opinions are not interpreted as lack of love.

My wife likes to look at clothes. I like to look at complicated watches.

We do both separately even though there is a great deal we also do together.

Occasionally, only when we feel like it, we do things we ordinarily do separately together. *But* we don't push each other to do it. We do not impose on each other.

People who love each other
seldom get bored with each other.

People are infinitely complex. There is always more to understand. Change always takes place involving still more understanding. People who love sustain interest and continue to pursue understanding—precluding boredom.

Boredom is the result of unused inner resources. People who love each other help each other to use their inner resources, their talents, their abilities effectively. This is an enormous antidote to boredom. Of course they do not blame each other for being bored and make no claims on each other to relieve boredom.

The compulsive need
of having to be repeatedly

told of being loved is not to be confused with the healthy desire to hear the words and their constructive effect.

The compulsive need can be most abrasive and eventually destructive to love.

The fear of rejection

prevents many of us from the attempt to initiate relationships that have the potential to be loving. This often occurs in people who desire to be loved by everyone all of the time.

Overcoming the fear by realizing that universal love is neither necessary, profitable, or possible and accepting rejection frees us to ask to be loved and to give love.

A love relationship cannot be continued for very long without accommodation because we are all arrhythmic.

This means that none of us always has the same needs and desires at the same time. To expect perfect synchronization is to expect the impossible. This could only happen if we were all duplicate copies of each other. This would lead to narcissistic preoccupation with duplicates of ourselves—the very opposite of love.

Differences enrich relationships and make cooperative, noncoercive accommodation a top priority.

There are two kinds of laughing.

One is destructive to love and invariably results in hurt feelings and often leads to retaliatory moves. It is sneering, derisive, sarcastic, demeaning, and just plain nasty. It is a perversion of healthy laughing. It has no connection to fun and is usually full of put-down vindictiveness, self-aggrandizement, and arrogance. Sometimes it seems to be related to laughing—a smile, really a sneer; a sound, really a snicker. Sometimes it is rationalized as laughing and follows statements like "Can't you take a joke?" or "Only kidding." But it isn't really laughing at all. It's bad stuff and everyone in its presence knows it and knows there's no love in it.

The other—the real thing, *laughing*—is letting go! It is open, hearty, honest, warm and usually involves our whole selves. This is the stuff of fun and a sure sign of joy—never at anyone's expense. It is almost always contagious and has the effect of lightening the load.

Unlike sneering, which leaves a foul residue or downright havoc in its wake, real laughing results in feeling good and feeling closer.

Simply put—laughing together is natural and constructive to loving people and especially to people who love each other. Laughing together is often still another expression of love.

Chronic concern about fair share,
equality, and fifty-fifty

is usually evidence of competitive relating.

In a loving, cooperative relationship each gives according to what he's got—receives according to what he needs.

I've heard that Sigmund Freud said

his mother called him "My golden Ziggy."

He said that he was able to accomplish what he did because of his mother's belief in him. He said that few people could resist self-realization and even greatness if parents believed in them.

The implication is that many people are not self-realized because of lack of parental belief in them.

I have had some patients who suffered because parents have had exorbitant expectations of them. But I've had many more patients who suffered because their parents had minimal or no expectations of them. This especially applies to women.

When I provided my (appropriate) expectations of them, which I consider a crucial form of love, they blossomed. In fact to date twenty of them who had minimal education and no such plan are now physicians, lawyers, psychologists, and psychoanalysts. Most of them are now psychiatrists themselves.

I believe there is much truth to the belief ascribed to Dr. Freud. But I believe that the parental influence is only valuable if the belief is a genuine one. This means that the hope and help for the child is not born of desires for vicarious glory. It means that there is no exploitation and that the child is accepted through times of failure as well as success.

In short, a parent's belief in a child and indeed an adult's belief in an adult can go a long way if it has a solid foundation of love.

Loving is more important than being loved.

The stronger our sense of self,

knowing who we are, how we feel, being in touch with our priorities in life, our values (what is and isn't important to us), and our goals, interests, and desires, the better equipped we are for loving.

This is so because with a full self we have so much more (of ourselves) to use in loving. This also makes for much less confusion and complications in relating. We are much clearer and more realistic about the persons we love.

Being strong selves makes us much more open and trusting and less guarded in both receiving and giving love. Minimal feelings of vulnerability here makes emotional investments and commitments easier.

Having a strong self must not be confused with selfishness. The former always includes care for others as well as self. Selfishness excludes both! The selfish person may seem to be self-caring but instead is usually self-absorbed. Without real interest in others, real self-interest isn't possible because the greatest self-nourishment as well as satisfaction in life comes from mutual caring, the basic stuff of adult love.

Selfishness, the antithesis of strong self, is born of poor self-esteem and a hazy concept of real self. Strong self is born of good self-esteem, real self-love, self-acceptance, and a realistic view of what it is to be a person in the real and current world.

Love is the great connector!

It connects each of us to the rest of humankind. As such it is a bulwark against the knowledge and fear of uncertainty, danger, and death itself.

When we are loving and connected, the knowledge that all persons, and especially people as a species, remain well and alive is a comfort to us. Then in a sense we stay alive also.

Love of someone
other than ourselves

can be an extremely powerful motivating device used for our own
good.

I have known many people I could only influence to stop drink-
ing, smoking, overeating, overworking, etc., by reminding them of
the continuing need loved ones had of them.

They started out doing it for a wife, a child, a friend, and
eventually did it for themselves.

Love's enemy #7: suspiciousness and paranoia

are extreme forms of jealousy. No amount of reassurance, no proof of innocence, no evidence, and no logic work here because the basis of this illness is self-hate. It has nothing to do with reality, so confrontation with reality is useless.

Not only is chronic suspiciousness and its even sicker brother—paranoia (distrust and fear of one's own projected self-hate)—destructive to love but it can also be life threatening. In these conditions, so-called loved ones are often soon seen as disappointing and even as dangerous enemies.

Love dilutes and even destroys hopelessness,

bitterness, cynicism, envy, vindictiveness, selfishness, chronic hostility, feelings of inadequacy, self-hate, intolerance, prejudice, arrogance, fear, and the whole host of human corrosives.

Love is the antidote and the healer even as these enemies are destructive to love.

The question is, which side do we serve? We must do what we can to devote ourselves to love rather than to hate so that the healer is not destroyed before it can heal.

When we deal with a person—
adult or child who, because of
damaging experiences can't seem
to love anymore, what can we do?

This is an only too common problem. Investigation usually reveals a person who has been badly enough hurt so that trust no longer exists.

Sometimes these people will trust only nonhumans.

Introducing these wounded people to a pet, particularly a loving puppy, can be very helpful. Few people can resist the love of a small dog. Once love germinates it keeps growing and can flourish sufficiently so as to risk new investment in people as a natural and easier process.

Of course time is important here and patience and sensitivity are a must.

Is love always sexually connected?

Love can be sexual or nonsexual.

Heterosexual men can love heterosexual men. Heterosexual women can love heterosexual women. I disagree with those Freudians who believe that there is always a sexual current or correlation present.

Why don't we see men express love for men to a greater extent?

A great many men see expressions of love, especially for other men, as a sign of femininity—and possibly homosexuality. These can be enormously threatening to feelings of identity and especially to the masculine image they have of themselves.

Much inhibition in this area comes from considerable confusion about heterosexual characteristics and homosexuality.

Homosexual people are more than attracted sexually to members of the same sex. They also develop emotional involvements and desire to live together just as heterosexuals do with members of the opposite sex.

We must keep in mind and convey to our children that: heterosexual men can feel, be poetic, can be passive, frightened, confused, cooperative, noncompetitive, dependent and, above all, loving. Heterosexual women can be independent, strong, assertive, angry, competitive, and all things human.

Kids who don't know this cut aspects of themselves off of themselves. This destroys creative ability, relating ability, and loving ability.

One of the painful aspects of love

is that it extends our vulnerability.

We have children and then they are out there—the most delicate parts of ourselves. Despite our confidence in them we have trepidation about their vulnerability because any wound to them hurts us in our most vital cores.

Arguing

can be a way of feeling and sharing love.

This often happens with men who need emotional friction to exchange love but who feel that more direct ways are less than masculine.

Arguing can be a way of sustaining contact. This may be a continuation of the bantering and horsing around so characteristic of friendly adolescent boys.

I lost my father twelve years ago.

We loved each other deeply and argued a great deal. I miss him. I miss the arguments. More than anything I miss the opportunity we both missed to tell of our love for each other in so many words.

Love is therapeutic, is aliveness,
is health, is meaning, is human

and as with all things human it is an exhorbitant expectation to believe that it solves all problems. But it sure helps!

Seeking and finding

some good in people we dislike or people whom society judges as "bad" exercises and increases our loving ability.

Love's enemy #8:
arbitrary rightness

simply means to have the compulsive need always—*always*—to be right. This often necessitates bending the truth and denying reality with absurd rationalizations.

The willingness to be wrong at least some of the time is an absolute necessity in love relationships.

This corrosive is particularly destructive to humility—a quality that makes loving so much easier.

The *always right* person cannot learn from mistakes, cannot accept criticism, and suffers from feelings of humiliation constantly. He projects these to people who try to love him. This person desperately needs humility in which we accept limits and assets, rights and wrongs, and cherish our ability to apologize where appropriate.

Love is a powerful alchemist!

Where there is love of work—work becomes play.

Where there is love, criticism that may otherwise have been received harshly is received graciously, openly, with trust.

Where there is love, envy turns to happiness for the other person's attainments.

People who find it difficult to take advice use it fruitfully if given with love.

Apathy and inertia can be converted by love (a loved mentor or muse) to high motivation and constructive action.

Love converts suspicion to trust.

The professional therapist demonstrates his love of the patient through compassionate acceptance and understanding. This love may initiate the conversion of the patient's self-hate to self-love and can help change depression into happiness.

Laughing is better than fighting.

Discussing is better than fighting.

Kissing and hugging is better than fighting.

Comforting is a lot better—whatever form it takes.

Helping—any kind, any form—is wonderful.

Understanding is great.

Playing is superb.

Doing-anything-together—just holding hands—is terrific stuff. Ever try to continue to fight while holding hands?

But if angry feelings are there and they don't go away—get them out—directly, warmly, cleanly! No hidden sabatoge! No sullen coldness! No abused feelings! No displacement to other people! No vindictive tirades! No isolating of self! No guilt engendering!

Get it out, over with, behind you, and make sure your partner has equal opportunity to do the same and listen respectfully when he/she sounds off.

Clear the air and then breathe deep and warm and feel good about self and each other and laugh and play!

When we love people

the fact that they are human comes first before their nationality, religion, gender, beliefs, looks, or any other identifying characteristics. We love them because they are people, because we love the human condition and accept it in all of its variations and richness.

From a mental health
point of view

I see love as a very special therapeutic agent, undoubtedly unique.

Love has the special power to make us feel together, whole, and good.

This feeling together and whole is, I believe, the result of love having an internal binding effect. This is so because when we love we are in touch with all aspects of ourselves. We are more accepting of all aspects of ourselves.

In the state of high morale, characteristic of feeling love, all aspects of ourselves are more alive as well as united. This feeling of wholeness, fullness, and vitality is a tonic for health on all levels but is a special boon to our mental health and state of well-being.

Love is no excuse to take anyone
for granted or for poor manners.

Indeed, sensitivity to needs, gracious behavior, good manners, and gratitude are expressions of love and especially appreciated by those whom we love.

Gratuitous or
unsolicited compliments
are nearly always appreciated.

This is not true of criticism.
But both may or may not come from feelings of love.

Love's enemy #9: arrogance

makes us truly unlovable and very difficult to get along with in just about any circumstance. This corrosive makes people attribute qualities to themselves, such as prestige, power, knowledge, assets, and exalted standing in all areas of life, often beyond human proportion and that they simply don't have. Unfortunately, they demand to be treated as if they do own all the properties they have arrogated to themselves.

As in arbitrary rightness and as in all cases when our image of ourselves has no basis in reality—abused reactions abound. These, plus the general abrasive effect of people without humility, makes it very difficult for love to flourish.

The real truth is that arrogance is used to cover up fear of great vulnerability born of low self-esteem and feelings of inadequacy. But the real truth remains, unconscious, buried by the cover-up of arrogance. Relationships and love suffer the consequence unless the individual can face the truth about himself.

Of course, the ultimate cure here is humility. This can come through love. Unfortunately, very arrogant people interpret love as weakness, as patronization, and as humiliation. They just can't believe they can be lovable, and usually decide that superiority is more valuable than love—thus depriving themselves of what they more than anyone need the most.

Of course the bargain is a disaster. Even their superiority is mythical and exists only in their own imaginations where they have arrogated to themselves nonexistent attributes.

I looked out the window.

An unexpected heavy rain had started. I left my umbrella at home.

I wondered if my wife would bring me an umbrella. I had a fleeting thought: *does she love me?* What if she didn't bring it?

Then I realized I was having an acute attack of unlovability—based on a frustrating experience with a patient that morning.

She brought me the umbrella. I hope I would have felt loved by her if she hadn't.

Love's enemy #10:
greed and stinginess.

All and every kind of greed and stinginess shrinks the soul, dries out life and love's vital juices and human relating power.

But in this context the particularly destructive kind of greed is wanting everything one's own way. No willingness to give up anything. No willingness to compromise. No willingness to share.

This enemy means being tight about giving of one's self. Doling out affection, help, support, admiration, feelings, information, ideas by thimblefuls at best.

If the condition is severe we are dealing with a person who is incapable of anything but one-way-street receiving—and this usually ungraciously. No exchange is possible here. Without change, love dries up as does the human soul.

when it is applied to what we do and to what we have—home, work, a walk, a meal, exercise, visiting, etc.—enriches and enlarges the object or action and ourselves.

When we love what we do we do not get bored, depressed, exhausted, angry, and demoralized.

Love of what we do for another person lifts the heart and makes everything lighter, brighter, and easier.

Looks—

superficial looks—a look—has great power to attract.

Loved ones like to see loved ones take care of themselves and that includes their looks. It also conveys the message of caring about the people who live with and look at us.

But as time goes on and love grows, looks are mostly important in the messages they convey about feelings of all kinds.

Replacement

of a loved one who has been lost often produces guilt. This comes from the unfortunate belief that the lost loved one has not been loved enough.

Too, often it is felt that fidelity to the love of one's lost partner can only be proven and demonstrated by lifelong solitude and mourning.

Actually, replacement is an indication of love for the lost one and demonstrates the attempt to transfer and to continue that love. It is also an indication of the love of life and the desire to live a long, full, loving life. This is further evidence of respect for the relationship that used to be.

Adolescents

who initially are embarrassed by their newfound strong feelings and an ineptitude in expressing them cover up by hostile ranking, bantering, and sarcasm.

It is unfortunate when this habit is continued into adulthood and the expression of love is made through wisecracks, sarcasm, and mutual expressions of hostility. Eventually, these kinds of expressions may create confusion and deterioration of a relationship. Where this exists it is important to recognize it and to make every effort to stop it.

It is also helpful for parents to tell adolescents and young adults that expressions of affection are usually welcome (where appropriate and especially where reciprocated) and even desirable, especially as people grow up.

is innate to those of us who have not been polluted by greed, narcissism, envy, and rage.

A sense of fairness is important to every relationship. It is absolutely essential to loving relationships.

Fairness comes from and is a measure of selflessness, sensitivity to other people's needs, good judgment, and the ability to empathize or to see things through other people's eyeglasses.

Help can be bought.

Care can be bought.
Support can be bought.
Loyalty of a sort can be bought.
Sex can be bought.
Sometimes even forms of openness, tenderness, intimacy, and trust can be bought.
Kindness can be bought.
But—love is much more than the sum of its parts. Love cannot be bought.

Love's enemy #11: getting even
or the need to get even

derives from and feeds adversary, competitive relating.

This dilutes and eventually destroys cooperation, a cornerstone of the love process.

Lovers are not interested in being even.

Lovers do not feel deprived by each other.

Lovers revel in what they can give each other. They find self-realization in aiding each other's self-realization.

Loving parents—that is,
parents who love each other,

influence children to love themselves and to love their brothers, sisters, and friends, too.

These children suffer from fewer internal conflicts and from less sibling rivalry and destructive competitive drives.

The children of loving parents have a much better chance at having good self-esteem and emotional security.

The children of parents who love each other inevitably have parents who love their children. These children tend to be at peace with themselves and others and usually find it easier to love.

we promote respect for ourselves and respect for others when we are practicing love.

When we make our own decisions we do this.

When we help people see choices they have in making decisions we are infinitely more loving than when we tell them what to do.

Of course it is true!

People who love, look better, feel better, and do everything better.

This is because they are in a better state of physical and emotional health.

They are in fact more alive and appropriately look and feel more alive and function accordingly.

"You seem to glow—are you in love?" is a justified observation and an appropriate question. We do glow when we love because our circulation is better, our skin quality and color is better, and our eyes are clearer.

We also look better, because feeling the way we do we take better care of ourselves—how we eat, drink, dress, exercise, and relax.

Love helps us to get a kick out of everything good in the world— the air, sunshine, rain, food—all of it, and in this way our mood and morale is elevated and we look accordingly.

*The better our opinion
is of ourselves,*

the higher our self-esteem, the more likely it is we know the difference between real love and empty words designed to manipulate.

But, there are very few of us, even the most adequate of us, who are not moved by real love.

Reality

is extremely valuable in love.

What I mean is this: When we love someone as he or she really is—faults, limits and all—love stands a much better chance of lasting.

To the extent that we idealize the person we love, we introduce possibility for disappointment and difficulty.

Therefore, it is very valuable to see ourselves and each other realistically. This in no way need dilute romance and is a definite enhancer of the real thing for the real person.

About gifts:

Just about all of us enjoy receiving and giving gifts. This applies to both men and women, though sometimes men are embarrassed by the process. This is particularly true of men whose macho confusion makes them embarrassed by strong, tender feelings, and especially of showing them.

A gift can be a wonderful symbolic gesture of love.

But this is true only if the gift is not loved more than the "loved one" and only if the gift is not used either as a manipulative bribe or to assuage feelings of guilt.

Sometimes receiving gifts and/or giving them becomes compulsory—by mandate. This is inevitably evidence of feelings of unlovability or a simple business transaction or both. In these cases the love symbolism of the gift (giving or receiving) is either minuscule or missing altogether. In these cases the result of the gift giving (the favor requested, the pseudoaffection given, compliance, etc.) is usually directly proportional to the cash value of the gift.

The most serious love gifts come in the form of help given, service donated, constructive advice, morale boosts. Love is further promoted when these are recognized for what they really are. They convey love as well or better than the most expensive trinkets.

Of course there is no gift like love itself, however it is conveyed.

When we give someone love—real love (openness, tenderness, intimacy, shared feelings, trust, caring, kindness) we give them the most and the best of ourselves. We know this because we feel so much better in doing it and we know how good we feel when we are given love.

The basic remedy
for most troubled couples

is for each to give more to the other. The basic difficulty is the self-deprivation that comes of not giving.

Giving makes us grow ten times more than receiving.

Self-esteem, so necessary to love, is best raised by developing the joy of nonmartyred giving. This is the best self-nourishment.

Love's enemy #12: manipulation

is often a child of malignant mastery, Love's enemy #26.

Manipulation, however rationalized, is invariably used to exploit for one's own selfish purpose and is not at all motivated by the desire for betterment of the partners or the partnership's status. Manipulation through production of guilt, martyrdom, and contrived suffering is particularly destructive.

It always makes for distrust, closure, and eventually chronic hostile feelings, all destroying the underpinnings of love.

Quantity and Quality.

There is no fixed fund of love—just so much and then it runs out. Love is better seen as a process rather than as a fixed, depletable supply.

Love in healthy people is generated all of their lives. There is always enough love for everyone they emotionally invest in—that is, care about.

Loving ability does not wear out. Old people are as capable of enjoying the process as the young.

Of course, intensity of feelings vary. We don't dedicate ourselves to everybody, and the quality of our love changes and becomes deeper as we share our lives with certain people.

When this sharing takes place in an exclusive one-and-only "in love" committed relationship, we make history together and a powerful bond and depth of feelings come into being.

Love relationships continue to change endlessly and grow. They never remain static. The love process is a creative one and people have an infinite capacity to share more and more as long as they live.

The deepest kind of love is more than a feeling. Emotionally committed people, or people "in love," create a special mood—an ambience of deep compassion for themselves and all that is human including the fact of our mortality. This brings joy and a certain sadness, too, for the reality of our finiteness and knowledge of our eventual loss. But in this "mood" we also create a unique and special language—words, gestures, and transmissions, which cannot be consciously perceived through which we perceive and share our deepest feelings from the most blatant to the most subtle, from the deepest concerns and fears to the most jubiliant joys.

Make no mistake about the "one and only" phenomenon. It is important, the dedication of one's self to an exclusive and uniquely special relationship makes the quality of love possible and initiates the start of the special language. This phenomenon does not happen as an outside bolt of lightning that strikes. It happens from the inside. What I mean is that it happens all of our lives together but begins only when we make it begin by making the great decision in our lives to commit to each other and to the *in love* process.

Respect for a child is surely
a crucial form of love.

Respect for his assets, limits, needs, unique characteristics, his feelings, ideas, self-expression, his right to emote, his proclivities, yearnings—this love will give him great strength in his future life as an adult.

Help!

To be able to ask for and to be able to accept help graciously when we need it is also an important form of love. How can it be otherwise when the giving and the taking of anything at all—all exchanges, all cooperative actions—are deep-down forms of human love?

But giving and accepting help is a very special form of love. It is love of ourselves and at its best it is also love of the person of whom we ask.

It often takes this kind of real self-dignifying love to put down sick and inhibiting pride and to put down the need for exaggerated and destructive independence.

One of the sickest and saddest statements (or its equivalent) I hear periodically is "I'd rather starve to death than ask for help." People who say this are invariably proud, closed, detached, and self-hating. They are in desperate need of love to open themselves up to the goodness inherent in being human and being with human beings.

*Imagination can be creative,
constructive, and fun.*

But some of us who live too much in our imaginations hold back
our love too long.

We wait and wait for "the right one" to come along and our
expectations are ever so high and out of reach. Imaginary people do
not produce love or adequate objects to love.

In this kind of waiting our ability to love can become frozen from
disuse until it virtually ceases to exist altogether.

For the patient to get benefit
from psychoanalytic psychotherapy

he must transfer feelings he has toward parents, brothers, and sisters to his therapist so they can be examined. The main ingredient of these feelings to be used beneficially is love.

Where there is no love to transfer, and no ability to invest emotions, and minimal or no relating taking place, the benefit to be gained from treatment is minimal or nil.

Love does not produce
exclusivity of attraction.

People are attracted to people no matter how much they are in love with one person.

But some people act out on their multiple attractions. Some committed people don't. I suspect this is largely what differentiates the boys from the men.

"If you love me

you will love and accept anything I do even if it hurts you" is of course a neurotic claim. The person who makes the claim is asking for universal and unconditional acceptance and love rather than adult love. We love people, we accept them with their faults—even grievous faults—but we do not love these faults.

The person making the claim does not do so on the basis of love but rather on the basis of greedy, infantile narcissism with utter disregard of one's fellows or their feelings.

My patient complained
that his wife is not open with him.

She conveys little of what she feels to him. He knows that openness is crucial to love.

I questioned him and it came out that he too is closed.

I suggested that *he* try openness—

Tell her about his complaints, fears, goals, feelings, desires, opinions, ideas. etc. Reveal who he really is!

The simple truth is that openness begets openness. There is no substitute for it. It is often irresistible.

Love's enemy #13:
hidden agendas

is a part of manipulation.

The person here rationalizes the attempt to have his way by verbalizing something that sounds and seems logical and "fair."

Actually though, he does what he does to get what he wants, which is part of a schema that is always hidden from view.

In other words—what you see *is not* what you get.

We all need people!

We need the sight, sound, smell, feel, and attention too, of each other.

Deprived of all sensory perception of people in isolation experiments or through accidents (shipwrecks) we hallucinate people's voices, sights, and smells and become delusional believing that nonexistent people are present. Our imaginations create fantasy people to fill the void and our innate, visceral need.

Old people desperately need people. Without them, they become silent, withdrawn, nonfunctioning, and die.

Infants need people. Without them they don't grow, regress, and even die.

All of us need people. Without them we become depressed and emotionally and intellectually stunted.

The major, most basic part, of this organic need for people is to love them and to be loved by them whatever subtle, simple, blatant, or complex form love takes.

A pet cannot take the place of people.

But a pet who loves and who provides a living creature to be loved can help prevent our loving and living ability from drying up and dying. Pets can contribute to happiness, health, and the prolongation of life.

*Martyrdom, self-effacement,
suffering, engendering guilt
in one's self, succumbing to
blackmail—these are never,
never evidence of love.*

They are signs of self-hate and neurotic dependency.

Living

for someone or for a cause or for a principle is almost always more significant in terms of love than dying for someone or a cause or a principle.

Living together

brings out the best and the worst in people.

Love is unique in helping us transcend the worst and to make the most of the best.

Hugging

is invaluable to our well-being—physically, emotionally, and mentally. This is especially true of old people who often appreciate hugs more than words.

Love does not diminish

the value and effectiveness of apology and gratitude. There is plenty of room for both in loving relationships.

Love's enemy #14: pride,

in which we puff ourselves up actually to protect ourselves against feeling inadequate, is perhaps the most destructive of love's enemies and intimately linked to all of them.

Pride presents us as images of who we want to be rather than our real selves. Proud selves are really a conglomerate of self-deluding affectations in which we arrogate to ourselves qualities we don't own.

Proud selves, unfortunately, lack humility, compassion, sensitivity, and the humanity necessary for love. Energy and vitality are used to keep us puffed up and feeling important and sustaining lies about our phony exalted status. If the truth of our human limitations is revealed, our pride is hurt and we are put in touch with feelings of inadequacy. This stirs up unbearable self-hate which is projected to loved ones. To restore pride we usually attempt to score vindictive triumphs or remove ourselves altogether, in effect saying that we need no one because we are powerful enough to get along on our own. This is "The hell with you—I'll take my marbles and go home," phenomenon. Obviously, all these mechanisms are highly destructive to honest love relationships.

Very proud people are extremely difficult to deal with—"Like walking on glass all the time." When we take pride in being all-kind, powerful, good, all-knowing, and in having sexual prowess, we are set up for an inevitable fall and make it very difficult to sustain love relationships.

Of course, when two people suffer from great pride, the going is especially rough. These people tend to get caught in pride deadlocks in which neither can seem to "give in." The admission of mutual limitations, humanity, and, where appropriate, wrongdoing, can work wonders here. *Apology* is absolutely a treasure in both breaking pride deadlocks and in generating humility. Unfortunately, some severely pride-ridden people view apology as humiliation rather than humility.

Forgiveness is invaluable here. It is a key characteristic of being human that helps eradicate hurt-pride feelings and aids the restoration of love. But, much more than forgiveness of each other, the real therapeutic power lies in the forgiveness of ourselves for being less than ideal, for being wrong at times, for being human. This kind of forgiveness leads to self-acceptance, acceptance of each other, and acceptance of the human condition—all contributing to the very foundation of love.

A *family*

is not a family without love.

At best, without love, it is people living together on a boarder house service exchange basis.

My patient complained that her children dropped in now and then, using her house as a hotel. Unfortunately, she was describing more than perfunctory, utilitarian visits. She was also telling about the dearth of love in her household over the years. The change from "hotel" status requires mutual involvement and caring that comes only with love.

There are many people

who are so afraid of dependency that they overcompensate with an enormous investment in being independent.

This can have a freezing effect on their potential for love. They maintain so much distance that getting really to know a person cannot take place and neither can love.

When we love, what is it we share?
What is it we communicate?

We share all kinds of things: our food, our knowledge, our skills, our services, our concerns, our problems, our responsibilities, our secrets.

We talk and tell each other all sorts of things—what we've done in the past and today. Whom we met. Where we went, etc.

But the important things we share and tell each other about are our feelings, especially: how we feel about ourselves; how we feel about each other, about other people; about issues, desires, needs, goals, ideas, priorities, values, decisions, plans. In short, we talk about our innermost selves—who we really are.

Adulation, total adoration,
and hero worship

are products of infatuation and the results of morbid dependency. This stuff is born of fragility and the need for a strong figure to lean on and to look to for direction.

Sychopants and disciples are not lovers.

Love requires mutual respect and equality of status.

Even people who love each other
do get unreasonable,

angry, hurt, sulky, frustrating, inappropriate, and downright foolish at times.

We are only human.

The above are not evidence of lack of love.

When people love, these bumps in the road pass even faster if
they are helpful and supportive of each other especially during
tough times.

Why do some people who love each other seem to hurt each other so much?

First, I want to say that people who don't love each other hurt each other much more than people who do. But what about those that do?

1. We are very vulnerable to each other's words and actions. This is so because love makes us and what we do so much more important to each other.

2. We tend to test loyalty too much. This comes from self-doubt, which creates feelings of unlovability.

3. Our expectations are too high, especially when we want our partner in love to compensate for all past hurts.

4. We make too many claims.

5. We take too much for granted.

6. Love draws us very close together, especially in a society influenced by the drive toward exaggerated togetherness. This makes communications more frequent and thus offers more possibility for understanding and some misunderstanding also.

7. People who love one another share many stressful experiences together. Sometimes stress generates self-hate that is so intolerable it is projected to a trusted loved one in an unconscious quest for relief.

Supportive words,

good advice, words of welcome, and acceptance are all messages of love. Unfortunately, we are not always open and tuned in enough to appreciate these gifts. When we are—the warmth that we feel is of a very special comforting quality.

Even without full conscious awareness this feeling can perk up our self-esteem and contribute significantly to constructive moves of all kinds. I've heard this expressed a number of times in this way or its equivalent: "Funny thing, after I'm with her something good happens to me—she must bring me luck."

In custody battles

I have heard acrimonious divorced people fight bitterly over custody of their children.

I've wondered—

are they fighting for who will bring the child up?
are they fighting for control of the child?
are they fighting for the right to love the child exclusively?
are they fighting for ownership?
are they using the child in an attempt to make each other suffer?

We don't need to own or even to be with someone all the time to love her or him. Indeed, real love encourages people, more than anything else, to own themselves. People, particularly kids, are not possessions. Possessing them destroys them.

Never
must love be a rationalization
for allowing ourselves to be abused.

Indeed, abuse by a so-called loved one usually stems from one or more sources unrelated to love.

These may include:

> sadomasochism
> severe dependency
> obsessive infatuation
> chronic arrogant vindictiveness
> serious mental illness including frank psychoses
> (insanity) and/or sociopathy (antisocial) behavior.

Love simply does not result in either abuse or sacrifice of personal dignity, identity, or integrity.

In fact, real love always has roots in self-love that includes self-protection and enhances and augments self-love. This invariably nourishes personal dignity.

Conquests have no relationship to love.

The initial surge of success excitement that comes of being accepted dissipates fast. Further seductions or conquests that are actually attempts at proofs of acceptability and narcissistic shots in the arm are needed with greater rapidity and in increasing numbers.

As with all addictions it becomes increasingly difficult to produce and to sustain highs.

In this activity there is little or no caring and no emotional investment, only a quest for selfish satisfaction of a need for reassurance. This bears no relationship to love any more than sexual prostitution does.

Compulsive conformity used in an attempt to be loved just doesn't work!

It is intimately linked to and indeed is an extension of love's enemy #28, self-effacement. This is so because it leads to a surrender of our own values and a healthy sense of individuality and good personal judgment, ingredients necessary for the exchange of real love.

Conformity is particularly dangerous to adolescents who often overevaluate popularity. Popularity is not love! It is shallow stuff at best and like notoriety brings very little in terms of substantial nourishment of self.

Too many lonely adolescents and young adults conform to the point of engaging in dangerous practices in order to be popular and liked. This often accounts for drug use, smoking, dangerous car racing, sexual acting out, etc.

"The right" looks, weight, job, clothes, and bank accounts can attract. They do not bring love.

Real self brings love! Affectations are a turnoff! Real self means real feelings, real values, real priorities, real concerns, real opinions, real desires, real choices, real interests, and above all real caring about other people and about one's real self.

Acceptance of our own humanity,

especially limitations, liabilities, confusions, wrongdoings, failures, and foibles makes it easier to accept and to be compassionate of others.

Compassion for self is almost always much more difficult to attain then compassion for others.

But once we do it—develop compassion for ourselves—we virtually guarantee compassion for others.

This more than lays the groundwork for love. It makes love a certainty!

Love's enemy #15:
duplicity and dishonesty

are quite simply the antithesis of openness and trust and destroy the possibility of real intimacy and loyalty. They always operate in concert with prideful self-deception, manipulation, and hidden agendas. They make for greedy exploitation and as such prevent any exchange of real feelings, or benevolent emotional investment characteristic of love.

*It is easier to
establish relationships
than to sustain them.*

Someone who cannot sustain relationships has serious difficulty with loving.

It is highly probable that at least several of love's enemies are at work here, and there is a desperate need to recognize them and to put them down.

When someone we love
is in a bad mood

we empathize and we help.

But we must not permit overidentification to spoil our own good mood so that we too slip into a bad mood.

We must retain our own separate selves and our own good mood.

With a strong self and a good mood we are much better able to help our partner out of his/her bad mood.

I have actually heard people say, "If you love me how can you feel so up when I feel so down?"

The answer ought to be "I love you. I love me. I love the mood I'm in. In this mood I can help you. It is better for you to feel as I do than for me to feel the way you do."

I am suspicious of so-called self-sacrifice in the service of love. I usually find that love produces maximum use of self to help a loved one. Unfortunately, much so-called self-sacrifice is often used to produce self-glorification through martyrdom and manipulation through the production of guilt. These are used to exploit the victim under the spurious guise of love. One of the saddest scenes is that of two such people vying with each other for position of greatest suffering.

and appreciate their children's love as much as children need parental love.

This is especially true when parents become older.

When parents get very old they need love in the form of care.

It is not unusual that somewhere along the line parents become the children and children become the parents. When this happens, hopefully they become benevolent parents. If they do, everyone will grow from the loving experience this brings them.

Stubbornness

is not quite an enemy but it comes close and makes things very difficult. It is just about always evidence of underlying feelings of fragility and vulnerability. This is the exact opposite of strength; however, in our society, stubbornness and rigidity are often confused with strength.

Stubbornness always gets in the way of love and much time and energy used to overcome this resistance to change is deflected from the love process.

Flexibility is born of strength. It smoothes the way—through ease of receptivity—for communicating feelings, ideas, thoughts, and preferences. It enhances openness. It encourages exchange.

In its most developed form, flexibility means the ability to graciously change one's ideas, where appropriate, with a sense of gain rather than loss.

Above all lovers are best friends.

Otherwise they may be sexual partners but are not lovers.

Dulling and avoiding emotional pain

by attempting not to care too much about anything or anybody is quite common.

People do this unconsciously, believing that detachment from serious involvement and "coolness" gives them personal independence, strength, and mainly protection from emotional entanglements and pain.

Unfortunately, this usually results in the pain of isolation and loneliness.

Mainly it results in life's major deprivation—that of love and its joys and benefits.

Is there a price to pay for involvement and commitment?

Of course there is! There is simply nothing in life for which we don't pay a price. Relationships invariably make for pain of adjustment, misunderstanding, frustration, disappointment, and loss. *But* the rewards here far outweigh the price.

What greater reward is there than living in the very center of life? Only love provides that center wherever and whoever we are.

Without love the very essence of life and who we are is missing. Without love our true potential is never realized. This price of noninvolvement for protection of potentially hurt feelings is much, much too high to pay.

All people do not require
equal time to feel love.

Some people generate feelings of love relatively quickly. Others require more time.

Familiarity can help!

We can get to love people we don't initially love or people we even dislike if we make the effort to get to know them and to understand them.

Love's enemy #16: competitiveness

is a prime ingredient of adversarial and antagonistic relating.

When you compete with a person you are concerned with betterment of your status compared to his or hers. Your standing takes precedence over his well-being. You use your energy to get ahead of her rather than to take care of her. Your interest is in being in charge rather than in cooperative relating between two healthy, independent adults.

This is simply the antithesis of creative relating and of love.

Suffering

is unfortunately necessary for some people in order to accept and to ask for love—especially for love in the form of help.

These are usually people who are severely prideful and who can only put down this pride with severe pain.

However prideful, people need love. Some of these people in unconscious desperation seek martyrdom, pain, and suffering as both a way of putting down pride and asking for love.

How much easier it would be to say, "I need your love," or to paraphrase "I need your help," rather than, "Look how desperate I am and how pained—I could use some loving help."

Doctors,

especially those who practice psychotherapy, ought to refer patients they don't like to other qualified physicians.

Patients must not be deprived of any aspect of the doctor's potential therapeutic contribution. This certainly includes therapeutic love (nonsexual of course).

I believe that despite the best intentions, lack of love on an unconscious level hampers motivation, limits creative output, and dulls perception.

With love, the doctor brings to the needy patient the full force of his therapeutic ability.

But more than anything, the patient invariably knows he is in the presence of someone who really cares and who is making a major investment in his well-being and in his getting well. This, combined with professional skill and talent, offers the best possibility for good therapeutic results.

Some people spill over with "feeling" constantly.

They use loving terms at the drop of a hat.

Too often, these expressions and terms are not in any way indications of either love or deep feelings. Indeed, when these people feel deeply, like the boy who cried wolf, it may be difficult to know that their expressions are hooked to the real thing.

There are people who have a difficult time demonstrating their feelings but who nevertheless feel and love deeply. Indeed some people are overwhelmed by feelings that are so intense they are rendered speechless.

Interestingly, some of the loudest "emoters" become particularly quiet when they feel deeply.

Some great lovers have difficulty articulating how they feel. Some highly articulate people do not love at all.

Rivalry

spoils real love relationships.

Those of us who have had strong rivalries with brothers and sisters in childhood must be especially careful not to transfer these feelings to mates and lovers.

Expressing love can be very difficult for adolescents.

Sometimes it starts out as bantering, put-downs, and teasing. Embarrassment is often due to confusion about strong feelings, vulnerability, and the fear of rejection.

To bridge the gap between bantering and true expressions of love may be very hard. Some of us drag this kind of thing—in the form of gratuitous sarcasm—as a burdensome accompaniment to love all of our lives.

Parents often confuse overpermissiveness and overprotection with love.

Unfortunately, these are born of parents' neurotic needs and not love of the child.

Overpermissiveness comes from an inability to take authority, uncertainty of one's abilities and judgment, and of being irresponsible and of being uncaring. The child suffers accordingly—feeling uncared for, unloved, and confused for lack of know-how and direction.

Overprotection is born of a parent's multiple anxieties and consists of one's own feeling of vulnerability and fear that is projected to the child.

This is one of the most crippling of influences! It stifles and constricts the child, making him/her feel weak and inadequate.

Love of a child in a healthy parent makes for an understanding of the child's real limits and assets and treating him accordingly. It also means helping her to realize her talents and to fulfill her potential.

If we love a child enough a certain amount of risk is inevitable because we desire, allow, and encourage her to be her own person and eventually to cross streets—alone.

Love requires commitment

to reach its full depths and amplitude and to activate and to develop its full pleasures and constructive value.

Lacking commitment, love remains a superficial, shallow thing, a spark that never bursts into flame.

Without commitment, love dies before it really begins to live fully and confers few of its potential rewards.

Commitment—dedication—provides one of love's most essential nutrients.

An "affair"

can be a sex affair, a love affair, or both.

In a sex affair—physical needs, pride needs, companionship needs may or may not be satisfied.

In a love affair with or without sex there is at least some degree present of the qualities that come under the umbrella of emotional investment. These include openness, trust, tenderness, caring, kindness, and intimacy in which feelings, ideas, goals, and values are shared.

A woman recently told me she
would give anything to have that
feeling again—to be able
to love someone.

In order to do this she must love herself again by giving up impossible standards collected over the years.

My patient said
he felt angry at everybody—

so much so that he couldn't love anyone.

It turned out that his expectations, claims, and subsequent disappointments were enormous.

We worked hard at reducing them to human standards. As we succeeded his feelings of love returned and eventually reached full amplitude.

People who love us

listen to us with great care and take what we say seriously. Therefore, it is very important to say what we do with care and seriousness.

We need people!

We do very poorly in isolation—so poor that in isolation experiments we hallucinate imaginary people in order not to be alone.

But what is it we need people for?

Is it merely a matter of exchange of needed services—mutual (healthy) practical interdependency? Is it a question of someone to play games with? Is it to keep from being lonely? I'm sure it is all of these things and all of them are very important.

But why do we deteriorate so quickly when we remove people from our lives? Why does our mental health and physical health too go into such sharp decline?

I believe it's because we must have people to love. The simple fact is that the loving process does not flourish in absentia. Without people we cannot exercise our love amply and that exercise is essential to our well-being.

We are, in fact, much more than cooperative creatures like ants and bees who also live in cooperative societies. We are, above all, loving creatures! We need to love as much as we need to eat. We can love objects, causes, and pets. But it is not enough. For the full amplitude of love necessary for our well-being to be realized, we need people to care about and to share with, to invest emotion in, to love. I believe that this, in large part, accounts for the marked increased in longevity in people who live in committed lives together even though there are other factors also.

Obsessive infatuation is not love!

A so called *crush* is really a form of self-involvement in which we project an idealized version of ourselves to the one on whom we have a crush. In this way, a crush can be seen as essentially being highly narcissistic since in effect we are infatuated with a projected image of ourselves. This is not love and can and usually does produce a kind of out-of-the-world sleepwalking nuttiness. It dulls and distorts our perceptions, affects our bodily functions, and can make us mildly ill.

Time is the most effective defense against making impulsive, destructive "love" commitments.

There is simply no substitute for really getting to know each other. This always takes time!

Despite immediate great mutual attraction and apparently having much in common, people are very complex beings. They need time to know each other deeply and even more time to see how they make out together.

Infatuations break up.

The pain comes from loss of excitement. This is especially painful for stimulation addicts.

Sex affairs break up. The pain can be great and the ensuing fights highly acrimonious, not out of lost love but out of hurt pride.

Dependency relationships break up. The pain here is largely that of terror of having "only" one's self to count on.

Real love affairs tend to go on and on as mutual exchange continues and commitment and caring deepens.

Love as with all things human
has its limits and does not
solve all problems.

But it certainly aids in their solution through good morale, increased strength of purpose, and effective cooperation.

When we love, I believe we are in a state of healing ourselves and others. I think this happens because in loving we bring together and tap so much that is good in ourselves.

Love makes us vital, energetic, "turned on and tuned in"—quite the contrary to being hazy, semiconscious, and loony, as songs and movies would have us believe. When we love, our glands, our organs, our tissues, our circulation, and our minds all work well. Our appetites are good; our judgment is good; our sleep is good and when we awake we are fully awake. We see, hear, smell, taste, feel, and think better and laugh more fully.

Love's enemy #17: secretiveness

is so often a form of hidden agendas, duplicity, and manipulation.

It is almost always a frontal attack on openness and intimacy characterized by a sharing of feelings.

Secrecy guarantees isolation and makes communication—so necessary for love to flourish—very difficult and often impossible.

There are secrets that are loving. These consist of information that, if gratutiously disclosed, would create great pain and even vast damage. But this is not to be confused with chronic secretiveness born of lack of trust and used to maintain domination and an arsenal of potential power and weapons.

Unfortunately, I have met many men who maintain much secrecy about money with the rationalization that they do not want to bother their wives with boring mundane matters. The real truth is that money is anything but mundane to them. The very men that keep these secrets regard money as their life's blood and the all-important identifying symbol of who and what they are in life. Secrets in this area are indications of lack of trust and a real unwillingness to share on a deep level.

This is the most common neurotic love equation.

It exists in different forms and often on an unconscious level out of awareness of its victim. It goes like this:

"If you love me you will also love all my shortcomings, excesses, irritating characteristics, childish demands, etc. You will make any and all sacrifices. If necessary you will surrender your own principles and all other priorities. This is proof of real love!" This is patently unrealistic and a perversion of love.

We may love each other but this in no way means that we love every aspect of each other unconditionally, nor does it mean unnecessary self-sacrifice in order to fulfill narcissistic demands.

Because we love each other we may accept each other's unlovable characteristics, but we must not expect to love them too.

The same is true of friends and relatives of loved ones. "Because I love you I may accept and tolerate people with whom you have relationships and accept your love of them. But should I not love them, this does not indicate a lack of love for you."

Having mutual interests, priorities, and desires are very helpful, but however much we love each other, our interests may at times be quite diverse.

To expect one hundred percent commonality and mutuality of preferences, appetites, desires, interests, and involvements invites disappointment and puts a strain on a loving relationship.

To make love

is a term that's OK. I use it, too. But I don't really believe we *make* love. We love and we express love.

Manipulating is always destructive!

But manipulation with sex as a reward or withholding sex as punishment soon destroys sex as an expression of love. Ultimately, as with manipulation generally, sexual manipulation destroys love in all its aspects.

People who have the misfortune
of feeling unlovable and undesirable
are enormously vulnerable to manipulation.

Many of these people fall in love with love.

They often victimize themselves by making great self-sacrificing moves as a reaction to empty words telling of love but used to manipulate. Of course, painful disappointment and feelings of abuse are the usual result.

I've seen this kind of suffering in all kinds of people, including those who are otherwise extremely sophisticated and worldly-wise.

A fair exchange
is no robbery,
but is not necessarily love either.

Many exchanges, including equitable exchanges, may be purely utilitarian and may lack emotional investment and personal caring (caring about the person with whom the exchange is made).

But if there is the beginning, even a small trace of trust, love—given a chance—may take root and develop. If this happens openness and more may follow, and love will then convert a relationship of convenience into a real friendship.

Teasing

as a kind of love jousting can be fun but can be dangerous too.

Teasing that becomes cloying, abrasive, and frustrating can lead to destructive rage reactions.

Mutual teasing that turns to adversarial one-upmanship is no longer playful and can turn love to vindictiveness.

If there is any history at all of teasing turning to fighting it is best not to tease—to stop as soon as it is recognized—which hopefully is as soon as it begins.

If teasing has become a habit, the couple involved ought to seek out their real, underlying areas of disgruntlement. They must stop converting anger to teasing and *have it out* constructively before they become real sadomasachistic antagonists.

Invidious relating destroys friendship and love!

The central purpose of this kind of relating is to generate envy in the other person.

This is done as an attempt to enhance one's own standing, accomplishments, and possessions.

This is usually accompanied by obnoxious bragging of one's own assets and disinterest in or putting down of the other person's assets.

Of course this is cancerous to love relating on any level and is the result of self-hate and feelings of inadequacy.

This kind of relating, if it lasts any time at all, receives equal contribution by both parties involved. It can go on for years, each person seeking to impress the other and both continuing to be deprived of real friendship and love.

Mutual morbid dependency

is often confused with love but usually lacks real, strong caring and warmth.

But what it always lacks is the nurturing of individual differences and needs.

Love binds, but not at each other's expense. In love, mutual, healthy dependency consists of mutual contribution commensurate with one's assets and abilities. Its main purpose is common betterment without dilution of individuality.

Neurotic dependency destroys individuality and freedom as each partner exploits and depletes the other in an insatiable and useless quest for feelings of security.

If, after being with certain people
who profess their love for us

we always feel "down," depleted, fatigued, angry, demoralized, and anxious, we had better examine the relationship. We may find it constructive and self-preserving and healthily self-loving to dilute or terminate it.

Chances are that "love" here unfortunately means exploitation, duplicity, manipulation, possessiveness, guilt production, inappropriate claims, and sadistic ploys and put-downs. However subtle and hidden these barbs may be, they are not the stuff of love.

Expressions of love in this case are used as cover-up camouflage and justification for exploitation and are really an insult to the most valuable emotion we own.

Parallel speaking
and real conversation.

There is a kind of conversation that I call *parallel speaking,* which leads to a sense of nonconnection, frustration, and "having nothing to say to each other." This is of course a spoiler of love.

In parallel speaking, each person goes on saying what he or she has to say by turn *without bouncing off each other.* It is as if he or she has his or her speech to make and waits politely or otherwise for the other to finish so that he can add to his own speech. This is not dialogue. No matter how much information is given and how well each person listens, this is not fruitful, love-enhancing conversation.

In real conversation, cross-associations constantly take place. This means that each time one person says something, the other person is stimulated by what is said, has associations to what is said, states them, and the first person does the same thing.

In other words, loving, involved people respond to each other's talk producing a common set of ideas to which each has contributed in response to each other.

This talk is an extension of feelings. These feelings and their expressions are inspired by each other in a real conversation—the antithesis of parallel speaking, which is isolated talk even though two people may be together and even listening.

Why are so many perfectly wonderful women often attracted to difficult, immature, and even cruel and sadistic men?

There is too often much confusion between cruelty and masculine strength. Actually, cruelty emanates from feelings of inadequacy and weakness. These are covered up by exaggerated but destructive macho affectations and acts that sometimes fool even the wisest women.

I am convinced

that there are far less disappointments with gentle, poetic, sensitive men as lovers than so called "macho" types.

However much we love,

none of us is in touch with loving feelings all of the time.

There are times when other feelings take precedence and are in the forefront of our consciousness.

But even though we may at times not be fully conscious of them we live our lives as loving people if we are loving. This means we go on caring, trusting, helping, etc., whether or not we are immediately conscious of loving.

can be highly destructive if it is carried on obsessively, indiscriminately, and with insensitivity to a love partner's feelings.

But please don't throw the baby out with the dirty bath water! Flirting can also be very useful and it can be very tough going without it. Most men in our society are terrified of rejection and will not make a move until they have been reassured by introductory signs of interest through flirtatious gestures.

Some shy people actually have to learn to flirt. Most of us without awareness learn from parents. Some people never experienced flirting because their parents stopped doing it (often unconsciously) before they were born.

Flirting is really a way of making contact. It is a way of saying, "I'm interested," and asking, "Are you?" It says, "Let's begin to know each other."

Flirting can serve as the opening phase of relationships that can be superficial and fleeting and of those that can turn out to be loving and of lifelong duration.

Flirting can take place with or without words, with a gesture, a glance, blatantly, or can be so subtle as to escape notice by everyone—even the people involved on a fully conscious level. Yet, however, it happens and regardless of consequences, usually at least some small indication of feeling and interest is conveyed. This can be very useful as the beginning of a love encounter.

Popularity is not the same as love

and doesn't have a thousandth of its value as a constructive force in life. Neither does notoriety. Both have been enormously exaggerated as routes to happiness in our celebrity-crazy society.

The simple fact is that any psychotherapist can tell you that a person can have a great notoriety, great prestige, stardom, and money—lots of it, too—and may still be miserable because of lack of a love relationship.

Passive people

in our society often confuse contempt, arrogance, and cruelty with strength and dependability. Of course they eventually find out the truth and come to realize that initial attraction can turn to hatred rather than love.

Cruelty is often also confused with masculinity and virility but is actually often the result of sexual inadequacy and serious sex problems.

Unfortunately, people who feel "dead and empty" often look for cruel treatment as a form of stimulation. They are so desperate to feel anything at all that they seek pain as stimulation and as much-needed attention. Of course this kind of attention is the absolute antithesis of love.

Fear of commitment

must not be perceived as lack of love.

There are people who are compulsively driven to stay clear of commitment. When they fall in love, they are thrown into deep conflict. In fact, the possibility of commitment makes them anxious and depressed.

Lack of love is not the problem here. More or greater love does not solve the problem. The problem is not a problem with love. The problem is terror of commitment, contract, and involvement. Love exacerbates the problem by producing internal conflict and anxiety.

The solution to the problem involves struggle and growing up. This sometimes requires professional psychotherapy.

Affection,

however it is shown—through words, hugs, gifts, or any gesture at all—is usually very well received and usually indicates liking or being liked even if only for the moment.

But a show of affection may or may not be connected to real feelings of love. When it is—it is particularly appreciated.

In general, as with the words "I love you"—for which, as I've said many times before, there is no substitute—it is best when our love, however strong, is not taken for granted. Gestures and symbols of affection prevent this from happening.

"I love you."

These words have enormous power. They can be reassuring, soothing, calming, healing, hope producing—pride, hate, and anguish dissolving—and uplifting.

Yet, these words are too often so difficult for many men to utter—toward lovers, children, friends, parents, brothers, and sisters. Why? Often because the words are a commitment to caring. Often, because of a fear of feeling and conveying that feeling to a loved one and the sense of open vulnerability this may bring. Often because of the destructive confusion in our society that this kind of expression is less than masculine and may indicate the beginning of being too feeling and less than masterful.

I wrote about this inhibition some years ago in the *Ladies' Home Journal*. I'm sorry to say that I don't feel the situation has changed appreciably.

I cannot stress enough the remedial value of these words—how much further they go than material gifts of any kind.

At first, saying these words may feel frightening—they are so revealing, committing, opening, and powerful. But the risk is more than just a little worthwhile. Of course I speak only of words that spring from genuine feelings and that are accompanied by appropriate cooperative human help and action. Simply put—it must be the real thing!

Manipulative, seductive game playing demeans these most meaningful words and puts those concerned at real risk of great damage.

The person who finally gets to it, breaks the inhibition, and utters the words may feel at first as if too much of himself has been given away. This may be anxiety provoking. But the anxiety dissipates and is followed by a feeling of satisfaction born of the most constructive kind of self-assertion. In saying these words we are experiencing, expressing, and asserting the richest, most serious, and important aspect of ourselves. This hugely enhances healthy, emotional self-growth and is evidence of adult investment of emotions in another human being.

This is also an affirmation that we realize loving is at least as important as being loved.

Too many people are so moved by expressions of love that they ignore how they feel about the other person. "I married him because he said he loved me."

The words "I love you" are an affirmation of active feelings about the other person. In a healthy, long relationship, both are there—being loved and loving.

Liking someone

is, I believe, a form of loving that person. I hear people say I love him but I don't like him, or I like him but I don't love him.

I believe that one can be infatuated, have a crush, and not like the person—and may not even know the person.

But I believe that liking a person is already evidence of love, even if it isn't deep and sustained love. I believe that our capacity to like one another initiates deeper love feelings, and when we love we do indeed like. This does not mean we like all aspects of each other. We may accept and love over all but there may be aspects we don't relish.

Love cannot be conjured up or forced.

If it's not there it is not there!

People in love with love often try to talk themselves into being in love with someone to whom they really are not at all attracted. This usually leads to disastrous consequences.

We simply can't change chemistry through willpower.

I've had patients who wanted to love a person because he was a very fine individual in all regards. But the motivation and the superb qualifications of the person could produce admiration, respect, and even affection, but not love.

Love is a feeling. Motivation to love and being open to love are wonderful. But love—the feeling—cannot be forced any more than wanting to like a particular food for which one has no taste.

The person or persons we come to have the strongest feelings for are not casual choices. The "choice" is made by a lifetime of developing into who we are and represents a very complex amalgam of lifelong experiences, values, esthetics, and all that constitutes our real selves.

We can accept with compassion and kindness and in this way love nearly any and every one. But deep love involving commitments and investments of ourselves on an exclusive basis is reserved for a person or persons in our lives is in no small part a natural consequence of who we are. This is not easily changed!

Love's enemy #18: rejection, vindictiveness, and vengeance

go hand in hand.

Arbitrary rejection is often a form of vindictive vengeance and the infliction of cruelty.

Regardless of form, vindictiveness (harsh recrimination, sabotage, sadistic acts) and rejection of a partner's needs, sensitivities, and characteristics are all the basis of antagonistic relating. This is the antithesis of love and is invariably corrosive to all concerned.

There is little as dehumanizing and devitalizing as vindictiveness and revenge.

The antidote is forgiveness—which is only possible with love.

Love provides infinitely richer communication but it does not provide instant communication.

Time, experience together, and healthy struggle are necessary in order to communicate our feelings and values to each other.

Again, I cannot stress enough that understanding without speech must not be taken for granted. There is simply no substitute for the spoken word. Talking is invaluable! Silence can be an enemy!

Eventually—but this takes time and history—"a love language" comes into being. This is a language developed between real lovers in which much meaning can be expressed in few words. But, again, this always takes time—time during which much talk does take place.

Yes, people who love each other
can at times be cruel and vindictive.

This can happen during a variety of overlapping conditions of which I found the following the most common.

1. In which self-hate is projected to a loved one.
2. In which anger at other people (a feared boss, a parent, a child) is displaced to one's partner in love.
3. When expectations run so high that mutual disappointment takes place.
4. When attacks of unlovability take place (business failure, helplessness) so that no amount of reassurance to the contrary is effective.
5. As temper tantrums due to high levels of frustration and anxiety in people having poor anxiety and frustration tolerance.
6. During periods of more than usual emotional depression.
7. When fear of loss, especially of a loved one (due to age, sickness or imminent danger) becomes accentuated.
8. When pride is hurt through any kind of hurt.
9. Due to alcohol or drug intoxication.
10. During physical and especially painful or frightening illness.
11. During periods of extreme fatigue.
12. Tension due to change of status quo—new job, new home, newborn child, etc.

Much depends on the maturity and mental health of the person in question. The more self-esteem that exists, the less frequently will vindictive attacks take place.

Through becoming
competitive adversaries

a great many love partners lose the sweetness and the love they have together. They seem to forget that they are not only on the same team—they *are* the team!

Winning over each other is losing all that is really worthwhile.

People who are highly competitive must be particularly careful in this regard. This especially applies to people engaged in highly competitive business outside the house. Bringing competition home to one's mate and children sows the seeds for disharmony and antagonism. I had a patient who had to periodically remind her husband, who was a lawyer, that she was not a lawyer fighting him and that they were not in court.

People who have a history of much competition and rivalry as kids with their brothers and sisters must be careful of displacements to their loved ones when they grow up.

Vacations with other couples

are often disastrous. Why?

So many friends are OK together until they move in together. Why?

And then, any number of people can live together in relative harmony until commitment takes place and "then it falls apart." Many of these people are too detached to tolerate commitment. Their overinvestment in freedom becomes so threatened by any step toward contractual commitment that it destroys the relationship.

But, I believe that even people who are not particularly detached need considerable love for each other to make it together for any length of time. When people have difficulty on vacations, they either have overestimated their love for each other or they have left their love at home. Unfamiliar places and circumstances can make us particularly anxious so that we need an extra supply of love to get along.

The fact persists that living together, being together, brings out the best and the worst in us. Only love helps us significantly to tolerate each other's foibles, eccentricities, and shortcomings.

Love's enemy #19: refusal to listen

deserves separate and special mention as a killer of love because it is the agent par excellence of frustration, torture, vindictiveness, and contempt. It is a surefire breaker of communication and destroyer of love.

It is particularly insidious and murderous when used during arguments in which one person sounds off and then turns his back and walks out before the other person can state his views or voice his feelings.

Even if agreement takes place at once—the opportunity for delivering the complete message must not be thwarted. If it is, this leads to festering frustration and warm anger is converted into chronic hostility.

Listening is, after all, the best way to dignify what the other person says and feels.

Love's enemy #20: narcissism

is not self-love.

In fact it has no connection to self-love and destroys the possibility of love of others.

Love of self, real self-esteem, invariably produces love of others, which in turn adds to self-esteem.

Narcissism is obsessive self-preoccupation to the exclusion of interest in, involvement with, or caring about anyone else. It is born of extreme lack of self-esteem and of being arrested at a very early stage of emotional development.

This condition destroys love for others or the possibility of love from others. Being deprived of real love kills the possibility of real love of self.

The total result of serious narcissism is isolation and self-corrosion.

*Love does not
completely dilute the pain
of insult and injustice.*

But injustice collecting and keeping lists of indiscretions corrodes love.

*Keeping mental lists
of collected hurts,*

grudges, indiscretions, wrongdoings, injustices, and mistakes—however real they are—become backbreaking burdens. They contribute to emotional breakdown, vindictiveness, bitterness, hostility, isolation, and depression. They make entry and acceptance of love where it is most needed very difficult.

Love's enemy #21: perfectionism is a love destroyer in at least several ways.

1. The partner to whom one can make an emotional commitment is never found because no such person exists, has ever existed, or will ever exist. Perfect people do not exist!

2. Perfect love does not exist.

3. Nothing in life is perfect! Only death is perfect and some people even have questions in this area. The human condition is perfectly imperfect and that goes for every one of us.

4. Perfectionists first idealize partners and then delude themselves into believing that they have indeed found the one person with perfect characteristics. Inevitable disappointment, acrimony, and hostility follow when the imperfect humanity of the fabricated ideal is discovered. These people are always hurt and angry at themselves, everyone else, and the world at large for making love impossible. With them the air is never cleared because new rage is regenerated before the old hostility is dissipated. This rage is an extremely effective block to love.

5. The perfectionistic partner increasingly becomes a tiresome, frustrating, burdensome corroder of morale who it is impossible to please and eventually to be with on any kind of constructive level.

*My patient complained that
his wife was always saying,
"Show me how much you love me,"
or its equivalent.*

He loves her. He admits that his demonstrations of love could be more frequent. He is in fact somewhat detached and not too good at showing his feeling.

But he also feels that she needs more than usual demonstrations of love.

"Constant reassurance." "She never has enough—presents, words, hugs, flowers,—guess she really can't believe it."

She probably doesn't. This usually comes from feelings of un-lovability—perhaps due to poor self-esteem, exorbitant expectations of self, etc.

The combination of this kind of person (probably somewhat dependent) to whom expressions of love have great relevance with a detached person who is supersensitive to coercion can bring much unhappiness to both.

One feels frustrated and in a chronic state of emotional hunger. The other feels coerced and depleted.

Both usually need help with their individual problems so as to function better together.

Love's enemy #22: claims,

especially those based on love—"If you love me, you will always—absolutely always be there for me"; "If you love me you will never, never forget anything I've said to you"; "If you loved me I wouldn't have to tell you—you would just know," etc., etc.—are highly abrasive, lead to rage, and are corrosive to all concerned.

Claims cannot be fulfilled and the person who makes them feels inappropriately abused. This leads to acrimonious accusations and vindictiveness—love killers for sure.

These are particularly prevalent in self-effacement, love's enemy #28. These people feel they are entitled to all kinds of special considerations based on their notions of (self-imposed) martyred self-sacrifice. "Because I suffer (my own doing), you owe me!"

What about crying together?

Do people who love each other cry together?

If they are intimate enough (and this takes more imtimacy than laughing together) they certainly do!

Crying together over a sentimental feeling, nostalgia, joy, loss, sadness, represents shared feelings—and shared feeling is of course the stuff of love. Some people—in love—would love to do it but unfortunately can only cry privately due to inhibitions usually involving macho confusion and the overriding pride in self-control.

When questioned about his lechery,

he said he just couldn't help himself—"I just love women so much, can't help touching them."

When questioned carefully, it came out that he loved the sensations he got from touching them but never knew a woman or women sufficiently well to love them.

Romance

is maudlin, foolish, and even an embarrassing affectation when it is not a vehicle for love.

When it is an extension of love it is a special and superb vehicle.

People who feel unlovable

are enormously vulnerable to flattery.

It is good to know that flattery is usually used to manipulate. This is not love!

The sixty-year-old man

told me he still could not find "the woman" to love.

My experience taught me that one or more of several conditions prevailed, none having anything at all to do with a shortage of excellent candidates. The difficulty was absolutely to be found in the man himself.

1. The man really did not want a relationship.
2. The man suffered from considerable lack of trust and even paranoia.
3. He is severely detached and terrified of commitment.
4. He is highly narcissistic and self-preoccupied to the exclusion of serious involvement with others.
5. He lives mainly in his imagination.
6. He is grossly immature and knows very little about human limitations.
7. He feels strongly unlovable.
8. This man is a severe perfectionist.
9. The man has much confusion about what constitutes love and loving relationships.
10. This man believes he will live forever.
11. The man suffers from the burden of many of love's enemies.

Love's enemy #23: cynicism, pessimism, bitterness, chronic distrust, and hopelessness

almost always go together and provide a mood that makes love impossible.

Love needs trust, openness, optimism, and hope. These feed love.

Bitterness and its confreres provide an emotional desert and dry love out of existence. Where they exist in force, they are inevitably signs of severe self-hate and emotional depression, often indicating need for professional help.

Many people
are chronically depressed

because there is no love in their lives and they no longer know that they are depressed or that they need love.

If you are trapped
in our society's youth cult

and need to stay young forever then you are the slave of time and will surely generate self-hate.

Making peace with the aging process increases love of self, love of the life process, and enhances aliveness and feelings of love generally.

To be needed

can be a form and expression of love, especially for old people in our society.

Love's enemy #24; gossip and the betrayal of confidences

are death to love for sure.

How can openness possibly be sustained with a chronic gossip? It can't! People who suffer from this affliction sometimes do it out of a need to express hidden hostility, envy, and feelings of being abused. Sometimes they do it in order to be viciously vengeful and on occasion they are conscious of the immediate satisfaction they feel. They are seldom conscious of the connection between their destructive gossip and the lack of love in their lives.

But most people gossip in order to give information, to be entertaining, to impress with self-importance so as to be liked, and in order to manipulate the receiver of their gift (gossip). But it doesn't work! Gossip destroys confidence and respect and people eventually know it for what it is.

Gossip is of course a prime destroyer of trust and trust is an integral part of love. Without trust love collapses.

Gossips are conscious of what they do. They know they are gossiping. However irresistible and compelling the need is—they can stop. They can break the habit and can establish the habit of keeping and cherishing confidences. Knowing that love is in fact being sacrificed in order to get fleeting satisfaction helps. Willpower helps. But if the gossip can't break the insidious habit alone it certainly pays to get professional psychotherapeutic help to do it.

My patient said, "I don't want to have sex. I want to make love."

To make love we must feel lovable and loving. Making love then makes us feel more lovable and loving and is considerably more gratifying than having sex.

Making love is almost never followed by a feeling of depletion, emptiness, or regret.

Can hate be changed to love?

Yes, but first the major change that must take place here is the recognition and dissolution of self-hate. Compassion for self must take the place of hate for self. This invariably takes considerable struggle for humility. The surrender of sick pride, perfectionistic standards (for self), sick self-glorification, and a readjustment to human standards must take place.

As this happens, competitive, adversarial, antagonistic relating gives way to cooperative relating.

The view and expectations of people other than ourselves must change to realistic proportions. Claims on them to be perfect, totally understanding, giving, loving, etc., must be fully recognized and relinquished.

May I suggest you read two books I wrote relative to this issue: *Compassion and Self-Hate* and *Reconciliations*.

Love's enemy #25:
chronic, inappropriate, and gratuitous criticism

is the result of combined perfectionism and vindictiveness.

However much this activity is rationalized with "I only want to help you" or its equivalents, it always serves as an everlasting corrosive to morale, esteem, and to love.

The chronic criticizer is a put-down artist; everyone knows it and eventually this joy killer is avoided like the plague.

"Why do they bother to stay together? They fight all the time!"

How often I've heard this question.

Sometimes they stay out of habit—inertia—because it's too hard to move, and also because the unfamiliar frightens them. Sometimes they stay out of sick mutual dependency.

And sometimes they stay out of love, even though their love may be hidden from those who witness their fights, and even from their own conscious selves. Unknown sometimes even to themselves, a loving kind of loyalty exists between them, covered up by habitual fighting that unfortunately has become their principal way of relating.

Parents who love each other

provide security and self-esteem for their children, which is the greatest bulwark against envy, jealousy, possessiveness, and just about all the rest of love's enemies.

Indeed, many of the enemies come from the insecurity of having had parents who did not have a stable, loving relationship.

In fact, much envy is rooted in wanting what other kids seem to have—namely, parents who love each other and who spend time loving their kids and their lives rather than bickering. Much envy in adult life is a displacement from this early time to wanting power, money, and trinkets that other people have. These are in fact love substitutes—which never take the place of a childhood household that lacked love.

So—loving each other is of course a major contribution to mental health, especially of children and to their future as adults.

People in love
may share a point of view.

In some issues they may have different points of view. Sometimes one person will change the mind of the other.

Sometimes they will retain their own separate points of view. *But* this does not drive them to go their separate ways! In fact they stay together, respect each other, and even more, they support their partner's right to stand on a different point of view even as they retain their own.

Love improves communication

as does practicing communicating and experiencing making ourselves understandable to each other again and again. Eventually understanding each other becomes easier.

But no matter how much people are in love, we are not mind readers.

There is simply no substitute—none!—for verbal language. This must be stressed! This also means telling each other our likes and dislikes. This is especially true of sex.

A word of caution—the time to talk about sexual problems and solutions is between sexual encounters, not during them.

In fact, all talk is better when timing is appropriate. The more difficult the problem, the better to talk it out when morale is high.

Love's enemy #26: mastery,

no matter how it is practiced, however benevolent—whether it is in relation to a lover, child, wife, business associate, etc.—is a form of exploitation and often blackmail.

"Do as I say and I'll give you this or that," in so many words or implied, is just plain no good!

We can *offer* direction but insisting on it (except with kids, but here, too, caution must be exercised not to direct for one's own needs) and manipulating to have our way, using overwhelming strength or force to insure it, is disrespectful of the other person's rights as an independent, free human being with unique personal characteristics. It is disastrous to self-realization and utterly destructive to love. An idol and a sychophant or disciple do not love each other. They usually represent mutual exploitation of one or another kind connected to severe mutual dependency.

Caring

is best demonstrated by concrete help and not by histrionics.

The capacity to love
is directly proportional to feeling lovable.

The language and expression of love

can be as beautiful as anything in this world. It can be moving and very important in its ameliorative effects, too.

But genuine help given as needed with compassion, grace, generosity, and respect, is the substance of love.

Even more than intellect

it is love that makes us unique on this planet.

I know about animal fidelity and yes, this may well be a kind of bonding, dependency love.

But I believe our species has a unique capacity to love that transcends bonding or dependency.

This kind of love is the giving of self for no reason other than the satisfaction of giving of self and for the contentment it brings. This is a unique and special generosity characteristic of human love, which is actually a form of human goodness.

This kind of love's generosity needs no recompense, no pat on the head, no tit-for-tat balance and no reward. It is in no way connected to self-aggrandizement disguised as martyrdom.

It springs from love of people and of the human condition. It springs from a sacred respect for life and nature in all forms, especially in the form of our species.

This kind of love and generous giving of self happens because it must happen. It happens as a natural consequence. Nothing contrived, compulsive, or unnatural impedes the natural flow. It is there because it is there and needs and has no other reason for being other than its being human.

In this kind of love—feelings, time, thoughts, and energy are given, are received, and are exchanged. *But* exchange is not the motivating force. Exchange takes place as a natural consequence; who gets more, less, or what, is of no consequence at all.

Love can exist without lust.
Lust can exist without love.
They can exist together.

Love's enemy #27: detachment, inattention, and neglect.

There are people who place freedom from involvement above all else. Maintaining distance is crucial for them. They do precious little with their so-called freedom but, nevertheless, are terribly threatened by closeness or potential commitment of any kind.

Being alone and desiring it sometimes is normal and constructive. But these people's detachment makes aloneness a way of life. When people who suffer this kind of withdrawal form "close" relationships, their partners, however self-sufficient they are, suffer the pain of inattention and neglect.

The simple fact is that we all require attention and caring. This is true for detached people too, which brings them to relationships and to anxiety-producing conflict with their need for freedom. This need usually starts early in life as a defense against being hurt, rejected, and neglected. Sadly, they inflict the same injury to a would-be loved one, destroying the possibility of love.

Many "friendships"

consist of adversarial, competitive relationships. I feel that real friendships are cooperative and for the most part mutually enhancing and loving.

I remember discussing the issue of helping others because it feels good with my father who was a great student of the Talmud.

If it feels good and this is a large part of the motivation in helping others, doesn't this constitute selfishness, I asked him?

My father said that he interpreted the Talmud as taking the view that personal motivation—feeling good or bad—was not central to the equation. The issue is decided by the result one desires. This means that if an action (regardless of motivation) is constructive and helpful to a friend, this constitutes love and goodness. If the motivating force is personal satisfaction, this does not detract from the love or goodness generated by help to the friend.

Years later, it struck me that for some people, personal satisfaction comes from vindictive triumph, sadistic ploys, destructive manipulations, and exploitation. For others, satisfaction comes from giving loving help.

To do for personal satisfaction is human, and for that satisfaction to be derived from aiding other people's well-being and self-realization is love.

Many relationships between adults

retain father/daughter and mother/son elements. There are some that contain both.

Despite some popular writing to the contrary, this is not necessarily awfully maladaptive.

In fact, many of us carry over at least some need for mothering and fathering—both active and passive roles—from childhood, despite considerable maturity.

When loving partners are happy to satisfy these needs in themselves and each other this can have a satisfying and even a constructive effect.

We ourselves make him or her "the one and only"!

This doesn't happen from the outside in but rather from the inside out. What I mean is that *we ourselves do it*. We designate! We make it happen! This takes time. The time is used to make the necessary emotional commitment and investment. It also takes dedication to and motivation for exclusivity. We chose the person! We invest ourselves in that person. We make that person, and only that person, the special one.

We then work at establishing history together and sustaining mutual *one and only* status. We no longer "shop around."

To give help when it is asked for is friendship!

To give appropriate help before it is asked for is love.

Love's enemy #28:
self-effacement and the compulsive
need to be universally loved
all the time.

Self-effacing people want love more than any others do. In fact, in seeing love as the solution to all human problems, they overinvest love and are always disappointed.

These people do anything and everything to be loved by everyone. They are like chameleons, changing constantly in an effort to please everyone. The main thing they do is to efface themselves in an effort to please everyone else in order to be loved by everyone all the time and to be safe. These superconformists unconsciously see love as the substance that will bind them to a self (the loved person) who will provide the better, stronger self they have surrendered to please everyone else.

These people glorify themselves as martyrs and attempt to generate guilt in others to manipulate them. They pride themselves on their extraordinary goodness and make enormous inappropriate claims on the basis of their goodness and love. Anger frightens them terribly since they feel this may prevent being liked. This makes for repression, displacement, confused messages, and duplicity.

This love is very often unfortunately a phony one used to absorb and to exploit for their own purposes—mainly to satisfy their enormous dependency. This dependency is largely due to the effacement of self. People who are always attempting to please everyone else eventually don't know who they are or what they feel and need other people to tell them. Unfortunately, when they seem to be loved they are not. What is being "loved" is the façade they are presenting. Therefore none of the benefits of real love accrue to them.

As I said before—we need a strong self with which to love and to give. Self-effacement destroys this possibility and real love. Instead it contributes to phony pseudoparasitic love, which is eventually abrasive enough to produce serious communication breakdown.

As I've said before, but it is so important in this connection I'll say it again:

We need a real self to be loved and to love with. This means real (our own) ideas, opinions, desires, goals, priorities, values, decisions, thoughts, and feelings that may or may not be those of other people.

My patient told me that he had loved many women in his time.

In time I found out that in fact he had had several infatuations; many "conquests," consisting of duplicitous, manipulative deceits; many short-lived sexual escapades of a convenience touch-and-run variety; several mutual morbid dependency encounters and a pathetically impoverished love life.

In fact, he had many so-called love affairs and virtually no experience at all with love or any of its important components such as kindness, intimacy, trust, openness, or caring. In his past "love affairs," the exchange of feelings and commitment were noticeably missing.

Love is a possibility

for just about all of us.

Prerequisities like IQ, special skills, money, beauty, etc., are not necessary.

But love requires attention, nurturing, and a fairly healthy mind.

If we can't do it we must have help. A loving person can sometimes help. If this is not possible or doesn't work, a good and loving professional therapist may help it to happen.

Please do not go to doctors who do not love people!

Please do not go to doctors who do not love practicing medicine! The risk is great. The price may be as high as life itself.

But fortunately the love of people and medicine usually go together.

Love's enemy #29: hate.

Anger is not the same as hate!

Anger is short-lived, warm, and is not related to vindictiveness. The message of displeasure is delivered. The air is cleared. The issue is finished and over with.

Hate is chronic, deep, abiding hostility that goes on and on spilling over and polluting all aspects of life. It is corrosive to self on all levels. It blocks and destroys all other feelings, especially love. It contributes to bitterness and cynicism. It aids suspicion, paranoia, and bigotry. It is a destroyer of health, morale, and creativity. More than anything, it cripples and distorts relationships making love and its therapeutic effect impossible.

The ability to love

is to me evidence of at least some emotional health.

Love relieves emotional depression.

Love can be a remarkable antianxiety agent and antidepressant.

Love of self dissipates self-hate—the essence of depression. Love of self can be generated by someone else loving us (the therapist's nonjudgmental compassion for her patient). But it can also be generated by our love for someone else.

I have talked elsewhere about a deeply depressed woman I knew in a hospital I worked in years ago. I insisted that she help another woman infinitely sicker and more helpless than herself. She did so even though it took great effort on her part. She fed the helpless woman, dressed her, washed her, talked to her. They both got better. The helper came out of her depression and left the hospital. All other efforts on the part of the staff had failed up to that point.

Love works here because it generates and feeds hope—the great bulwark against the depressed state of mine.

Love's enemy #30: lies.

Lies are disastrous to trust and trust is an integral part of love. Therefore lies always destroy love. Dishonesty is disrespectful of a love relationship. Love requires respect and openness and trust. Honesty makes these happen.

But this does not mean that gratuitous confessions that inflict great pain are appropriate and valuable. The truth can be used as a particularly cruel and vindictive tool of derision. Used in that way (e.g., telling a truly homely person how ugly he is) can be as harmful to love as lies.

Ebbs and flows are characteristic
of all feelings, love too.

Love is sometimes felt more strongly, sometimes less.

As I've said earlier, even if it isn't being felt full force, it is there waiting to be felt in greater amplitude at a more propitious time.

But taking the time helps to feel love fully. Sometimes this requires stopping other activities long enough to feel what we feel without diversion or dilution.

It can be revealing, therapeutic, and pleasurable to be quiet enough with ourselves periodically so that we feel what we feel with full conscious awareness.

Intensity of sexual feelings
or excitation

may or may not be related to love. Unfamiliarity and newness may produce a great deal of excitement having nothing at all to do with love.

The issue of the relationship of love and sexual excitation is important enough so that it deserves some detailed discussion here.

It is indeed unfortunate how many people view a lessening of sexual excitement as loss of love, lack of love, or "falling out of love." The fact is that sexual excitation may decrease with any number of factors including physical disability, fatigue, excessive worry, depression, routine living lacking ample holidays and change, and so on.

The claim on love here, as well as on one's love partner, is that a sexual high should be sustained endlessly. Many people split on this basis and seek other partners to provide the constant sexual high. Of course their disappointment is in fact the only thing sustained as each succeeding relationship becomes familiar and then falls apart.

This is not to say that love relationships do not have their periods of great sexual excitements. They do—very often when romance is introduced to interrupt the mundane and when vacation and change dilute everyday cares and responsibilities. There is no question that good sex is fed by an effort to be romantic partners as well as partners in everyday household problems and chores. There is no question that taking each other for granted is bad for romance.

But, it is important to realize that while the unfamiliar, change, may be very stimulating and exciting, the familiar can also add much to sexually fulfilling lives.

The familiar can be safe, secure, warm, and can bring with it much experience as well as artful creativity learned through years together. Personal history together can teach us what each of us likes and dislikes, to what and how we respond. We can, as a team, make much use of this knowledge in a continuing and growing sexual, love encounter. Sexual response to each other can become a habit, a good habit. This means that sexual excitation and satisfaction can become easier and increasingly natural. In other words, doing it together makes it easier and still better to do together. But the effort is worthwhile to keep sex from becoming routine, mechanical, and perfunctory. Indeed, we do well to keep all areas of life from becoming dully routine. Encouraging creative efforts; periodic changes of scene; extending interests (museums, books, plays, music); making new friends; helping others; all help immensely.

Even more important, love produces much more than sexual excitation. It makes possible a sexual encounter that is deeper in feelings, that brings on a more wholistic excitement that is global in its effect.

Another way of saying this is the following:

An unfamiliar sexual encounter can bring great excitement. When the encounter is over it is over! If there are succeeding encounters—as familiarity takes place—the excitement will become less intense and eventually will be of shallow intensity or consequence. The same is true of excitement produced by "conquest," which dissipates even faster with each succeeding conquest.

The deep feelings of the love/sex encounter grow in depth as it is repeated. Even more important, the feelings generated by the encounter are not dissipated and over with after each episode. On the contrary, they are intensified! These feelings, largely of contentment, are contributed back to the whole relationship of the lovers and make them feel even more loving. This means they become more aware of their openness, tender feelings, intimate feelings, and caring.

This may well be the reason that in nonloving sex, the sexers (as differentiated from lovers) often can't wait to get away from each other each time sex is over. There's no reason to stay!

In love/sex encounters, the lovers, following sex, desire more than ever to be together because their many feelings for each other are felt very strongly now and can be expressed by sustained closeness.

My patient said,

"Sometimes I love him and sometimes I don't but I am always in love with him."

When I questioned her further I found out that what she meant was this:

Moods and feelings change. We get sad. We get angry. We get happy.

Sometimes we are in touch with our loving feelings but at other times they are out of reach. But this does not mean they are not there.

"In love" to my patient means that her caring, her loyalty, her deep emotional investment is always there. Her feeling of love—that special sense of tender closeness, that feeling of warm melding—is sometimes there.

When it is temporarily shut off she knows this is not forever. She makes no decisions based on this temporary shut off. It does not alter their status at all. She knows that she continues to be "in love" with him.

She knows her feelings of love will return.

Love and life have sad phases too

—as when a loved one dies and real loss takes place.

But I believe in living life fully in all areas—especially love—even though this, for all of us who are mortal, inevitably means loss.

If in the attempt to avoid the pain of loss a loveless life has been led, the loss is even greater because in effect a lifeless life has been led.

But what about the love pain so many songs tell us about—unrequited, one-sided love? This is very painful and often occurs in adolescents who, incidentally, buy most of these records. Most of this is not, I suspect, love at all.

This is the stuff of crushes and obsessive infatuations in which people are in love with love and often never get to really know the object of their "love" at all. That person is usually a projected idealized version of themselves and has little or nothing to do with real live and normally limited people.

Make no mistake about it!

In love there is friendship with or without erotic implications. In friendship there is love. Indeed, as has been pointed out, there can be strong erotic encounters and no friendship—and that is *not* love!

Friendship varies from superficial to profound, from light to ultraserious. Here too, much depends on the degree of openness, trust, sharing, and caring.

Friendship needs at least some degree of optimistic openness and willingness to take a chance with closeness, even though periodic frustrations and hurts must take place.

People are simply not perfect creatures of communication. The struggle to communicate better and better is a lot of what friendship and love are all about.

Friendship always involves at least some mutual exchange (equal exchange is no issue). We are not selfish if we want attention, warmth, and caring provided we are willing to give, too, and know there are human limitations to giving.

Exorbitant expectations of friendship—of love, of people, of ourselves—are disastrous. Loving friends do not *always* remember; do not *always* give; are not *always* sensitive to our vulnerabilities; do not *always* prefer each other's company; are not *always* sympathetic; do not *always* want to listen. But eventually they come around and provide at least some of the above, some of the time.

Enhancing and sharing the joy
of each other's self-realization

is, I believe, one of the deepest and most gratifying and enriching forms of love. This means sharing the joy of each other's continuing healthy change and growth as potential proclivities and assets come to fruition.

This means special joy in the flowering of each other's creative enterprise. This means shared creative as well as individual creative work. The term I use to describe this kind of deeply felt loving is *creative relating*.

*Kindness is one
of the best forms of love*

and being kind is also a way of making love.

Cruelty can at times stimulate sexual excitement but cruelty eventually dulls the senses and destroys love. It invariably depletes and weakens the self as it hurts health on every level and can make us very sick.

*Many people do not know
that feelings of tenderness*

can initiate the strongest sexual desire, excitation, and response.

Love can soothe all kinds of hurts

and as such is one of nature's greatest healers.

Loving couples have an enormous ability to soothe each other. This can reduce stress significantly and in so doing can be lifesaving.

The state of feeling love is in itself life enhancing, life motivating, and life prolonging.

The desire to be alone

now and then is no evidence at all of lack of love. In fact it can be self-replenishing and can aid the love process.

The desire to be alone most of the time is due to considerable detachment and self-preoccupation and can be love destructive.

Love's enemy #31:
I want what I want when I want it.

This is a kind of malignant childishness that makes for utter lack of consideration for others.

In addition to a high degree of narcissism, people suffering from this corrosive to love have poor frustration tolerance, utter lack of patience, and marked insensitivity to the needs of others.

Love brings joy and pain.

The pain of loss is real indeed and especially so when we lose a loved one and find we are mortal after all.

But—love contributes to joy as nothing else in life can.

I've come to believe joy is largely what life is all about. But joy is only joy when its main base is love. This means that joy has constructive value only if it comes from constructive roots. I believe sustained joy comes mostly from serious encounters with work, causes, all kinds of involvements, and especially with meaningful relationships.

The highs of sadistic manipulation, mastery of others, pride puffs, exploitation, vindictive triumphs, are neither loving nor joyous.

for each other's unique characteristics, idiosyncrasies, need for privacy, and individuality is worth its weight in love.

Even the closest lovers and loving friends must not seek and must prevent melding into a grotesque single unit.

As I've said many times—and it is particularly applicable when we discuss friendship and love:

There are times we prefer other people's company and there are times we prefer to be alone. There are times each of us prefers to do different things. This is in no way evidence of lack of love or mutuality.

Good friends respect each other's individual needs and do not insist on exclusivity of attention. They share a great deal but insistence on sharing all feelings and all things creates stifling pressure.

Remember, human beings are arrhythmic—different appetites for different things at different times. Accommodation is necessary and so is occasional *separateness*. The people who push for constant compulsive togetherness are pushing coercion that results both in stifling individual spontaneity and in suffocating love and destroying it.

Having had the experience of being loved as a child

is an enormous contribution to feeling love as an adult.

But when this is missing I believe love is still possible—if motivation is high, struggle takes place, and especially if a relationship with the "right" person is initiated. The "right" person here is a person who has experienced being loved sometime in life and especially so if this has taken place in childhood.

There is an inner beauty

and when we love people we see it in the expression in their eyes, in their touch, in the vulnerability that comes through around the mouth and in all we perceive beneath the surface. That beauty lasts forever.

When we get older

we must not initiate a nonloving self-fulfilling prophecy. We must not talk ourselves or allow anyone else to talk us into settling for a nonloving existence.

People, whatever their age, retain their capacity for loving and aged people need love at least as much as when they were young. Remember, treating one's self well is a form of love!

When people resign from loving relationships, whatever their age, this is certain evidence of resignation from life itself. Love can be and must be demonstratively instituted by those around them. If this is not done, deep depression, hopelessness, premature (non-organic) senility and even early death may follow. If efforts made succeed in generating love, the beneficial results can be dramatic and inspiring.

Love in this connection applies mainly to people.

But even love of inanimate objects, causes, activities, nature, sports, and any and all things life has to offer helps. I believe very strongly that love in any and all forms slows the aging process and in any case makes the infirmities and limitations of advanced age infinitely more bearable. I should mention that this of course also applies to people suffering from any infirmity either of a short-lived nature or chronic illness. And this especially applies to all of us during periods of great stress, personal loss, or times of serious and difficult problems.

I cannot stress enough this simple belief that more and more I feel is a fact. Love prolongs, protects, and enhances life, health, and vitality. It also makes the unbearable and impossible bearable and possible, often contributing more than any other factor to worthwhile survival.

"Taking a chance on love."

How well I remember the song's moving words.

We do take chances when we love. We feel more—more of the joys and sadnessess, too. Our responsivity to everything in life is heightened along with our aliveness.

Alas, we are mortal. We don't live forever. Loved ones die.

The more wonderful anything is, the more painful the loss. But the lifelong sweet residue of fulfillment is wonderful too.

The song knew. Life is to be lived and loving is the best part of living, however vulnerable we become when we take that chance.

With love
life inevitably takes on meaning and focus.

Self-identification becomes strengthened. Priorities become clearer. A sense of proportion develops. Existing becomes real living.

With love to light the path
I make my way through life.